AWAKENING

AWAKENING
FINDING THE REST OF YOURSELF

JACOB GOODSON

PALMETTO
PUBLISHING
Charleston, SC
www.PalmettoPublishing.com

Copyright © 2024 by Jacob Goodson

All rights reserved

No portion of this book may be reproduced, stored in a retrieval system, or transmitted in any form by any means–electronic, mechanical, photocopy, recording, or other–except for brief quotations in printed reviews, without prior permission of the author.

Hardcover ISBN: 979-8-8229-4608-8
Paperback ISBN: 979-8-8229-4609-5

CONTENTS

Introduction 1

I	Beyond Operating	3
II	Filters	10
III	Transcendence	14
IV	Fear of change	19
V	The Great Act	25
VI	Opening the Heart to Truth	33
VII	Developing the Beginner's Path	37
VIII	The Pathless Path	42
IX	Foundations of Flow	48
X	The Hero's Journey	54
XI	Spiritual Bypassing	60
XII	Duality	65
XIII	Awakening the Etheric Heartbeat	71
XIV	Fundamentals of Shadow Work	78
XV	Meditation Tools	87
XVI	Summary	90

About the Author 93

Introduction

Who are you? I do not mean your name; I do not mean what you do; I am not after understanding what you own or possess or even what external skills you believe yourself to have mastered. I am simply interested in *who* you are. I am interested in the parts that have been buried; I am interested in why you have the beliefs that you have. In this modern society, within which we live and exist (at least partially), it is quite simple to see and understand the effects of social conditioning on the unconscious mind. We strive to fit in, and we love to be liked by all—and accepted by all. When we are not accepted, we are sad, depressed, and defeated, and our first thought is, "What can I change or transform about myself to make others like me?" Sadly this unconscious conditioning does not solely exist within the confines and limitations of an external society. It has found its way into the familial structure. Since birth, we were forced by parental figures to believe and act as they saw fit for our lives. Everything from religion to what we wear was decided for us from such a young age. We were hopelessly dependent on the notion that they would do what was best for us. Did they? Have they? A question: If you could have had the developed cerebral capacity and vernacular of an adult when you were a small child, do you think you would have made all of the same choices that your parental figures made for you that made you into who you are now? If you'd had a fully developed mind as a newborn, can you guarantee that you would have chosen the same religion or belief structure that you have now? Maybe you would still choose the same. Or maybe you wouldn't. Maybe you would've chosen Hinduism or Taoism, maybe the Buddhist culture would've suited you best. The point to take here is that since birth, we have been told who we must be, rather than being able to explore the possibilities of who we could've created ourselves to be. Here lies our mission for the duration of these pages: to dive deep within ourselves with honesty, beyond all conditioning, to connect with the parts of ourselves that have been forgotten or never experienced because of decades and centuries of societal and generational conditioning. As we venture on through this writing, I invite and encourage you to be like the newborn; as you read this, be the blank slate.

Follow along with these words as if you have not been taught a thing in life yet. This will assist in maintaining the most open mind possible. To make it ever so clear, there are countless possible facets to the disconnect we have within ourselves. This disconnect has built a society based off of fear and inauthenticity. When we have a society based on negative foundations such as these, the human ego takes control of society's trajectory, and we are left with an abundance of division, separation, fighting, war, power struggles, and so on, as we see in our world today. The fact of the matter is that inside each of us is the key to changing this world. Compassionate connection to ourselves breeds compassionate connection to all life, even to those we view as different and to those we don't understand. We have allowed concepts such as politics to divide us, and foster within us anger, resentment, and hatred toward our opponents, not realizing the simple truth: that we are all one being, and to fight others is to fight ourselves. Separation is humanity's greatest illusion. All of us are but different fingers of the same hand, asleep and unaware of the connection that we actually have to each other and all life on this planet—and on any other.

I

Beyond Operating

"Out beyond the ideas of wrongdoing and right doing, there is a field. I will meet you there." This is a line from the great poet, philosopher, and mystic Rumi. It will serve us well as a starting point as we begin to take the deep inhale into transcendence through our time together here.

So, why is this line so fundamental? Well, if it isn't obvious by its wording, let's break it down together. "Out beyond the ideas of wrongdoing and right doing"—let's start here. Rumi is first bringing awareness to the concepts of "right" and "wrong." It is crucial that we understand that the concepts of right and wrong change and vary and are a subject of perspective. The elephant parable may serve to prove this point. Several people were blindfolded and asked to touch a different part of an elephant.

The person touching the leg describes the elephant as a tree. The one touching the tail describes the elephant as a rope. The one touching the tusk describes the elephant as a spear. The one touching the side of the animal describes the elephant to be like a wall. They are each of them correct and incorrect at the same time. As humans, we have become so lost in our own individual experience that at times we forget that there are other people with different perspectives having a different experience that is just as real as our own. These are people with beliefs, upbringings, philosophies, and creeds that are different from ours, but they are still just as real to them as ours are to us.

This brings us to the next part of Rumi's line: "There is a field. I will meet you there." In this segment, Rumi offers us a third option that is other than right or wrong. The field he is speaking of is simply the awareness and understanding that there is no such thing as right or wrong. There is only the differentiation of perspective. In this world, there are many situations and events that are seen as problematic or negative to some, but to others they are seen as positive or the solution. As with the myriad of "problems" in this world, and the differentiation between perspectives, there is a slew of presented ideas and solutions to world situations. So how do we decide what solution to use? Who do we listen to? Do we vote? Do we fight? Do we go to war? Do we gamble? Do we steal? Do we sit and argue for hours upon end with little to no result? The answer? There is no answer here. This is the field of transcendental awareness that Rumi speaks of. There is no right or wrong way to resolve a scenario.

As humans, we will inevitably end up in disagreement because as humans we again have different upbringings and beliefs that have conditioned us to react and respond in certain ways to situations that occur in society. This again brings us to the importance of the transcendental journey of the self. When we learn to transcend our individual human belief systems, when we learn to transcend our indoctrination that has kept us unconscious since childhood, when we can accept the fact that nothing we are doing is working because both sides are stuck believing that they are "right," when we can accept these hard truths and begin to venture outside of the box, we will have begun the path to transcendence as a society. We will have begun the path to illumination.

"The definition of insanity is doing the same thing over and over and expecting different results." —Albert Einstein

This quote by Einstein is of the utmost importance in our world today. We have allowed ourselves to become divided, and through our delusion of separateness, we have established "teams" or "sides" and we have further deluded ourselves into believing that our side will be the one to finally bring peace and unity to the world. Do you see it? Do you see the delusion with this mindset? How could it ever be possible for a system based on sides and separation to be used as a foundation for unification? This brings us again back to Einstein's quote. We as a society have been attempting the same path for entire generations, and things only seem to shatter further and divide further, causing more negatively oriented situations as we again see in our world now. The inevitable conclusion that we will come to is that we must try something new in order to achieve a new or different result. Simply, if you want something new, you must do something new. It is solely out of ego and fear of the unknown that humanity refuses to accept and make the leap of faith into new and unexplored territory. Whether we realize this truth in one year or one hundred years, the delusion of separation must fall away if we are to unify our world based on truth.

These pages exist in the hope of assisting in the undoing of this great fear of the unknown, enabling us to surpass our mental limitations and experience an evolution of the self and an evolution of the collective at the mental and metaphysical levels. There are a great many analogies to be made that can make the illusion of sides, separation, politics, or anything having to do with opposing groups plain to see. The entirety of this struggle is the same as saying that a peanut butter and jelly sandwich can be made with one and not the other. Each side believes that they hold the key to the future, or the key to the only door, when in fact there is no door. Or rather, you might say, we are the door. We must only walk through and explore the depths of ourselves to begin to peer into divine truth and wisdom. As humans, we do not like great change. In fact, most times, we hate and reject change with our entire strength. We would rather stay comfortable than take the necessary accountability to create what we desire to see and experience in our world. It is crucial to understand that only when we accept the fact that what we have been trying is not working can we begin to ask the question "What can we try instead?"

This illusion of sides can be understood to a deeper extent with the knowing of the concept of duality. We will go deeper into duality later on; here it will be kept brief, simply to assist with this point. Duality is a fundamental term in esoteric communities for understanding the foundation of this illusion that is perceived separateness. Duality is essentially the polarization of opposite and nearly equal forces coming into play with each other. Simple examples of duality that we all are familiar with are dark vs. light, good vs. evil, love vs. hate, and up vs. down. The list goes on. It is imperative that when exploring the illusory nature of duality, we know that it is in fact an illusion of perception. There is no darkness without light; there is no knowledge of good if we do not know of the bad. We cannot know the concept of right if we do not have a contrast of something we perceive to be wrong. These examples are all parts to a greater whole, two parts of the same coin.

All parts are needed; we cannot know one without the contrast of the other. We believe these things to be separate only because of the limitations of human perception. This again points us toward the importance of transcendental practices, such as meditation or yoga. How does this relate to meditation or other spiritual practices? States of meditation can also be described as states of purity, or states of infinite awareness. This awareness is that of a level far beyond the limitations of human awareness. When we spend extended time in deep states of stillness and pure energetic awareness, we begin to connect with divine wisdom. We begin to connect with the true subtle flow of all creation, and we can bring this wisdom back into our waking physical lives. This is the word and wisdom of God. Now a disclaimer: whenever I use the term "God" in this book, I am not referring to any religion in particular, I am simply referring to the divine frequency, or blueprint if you will, that exists within and around all things. Including us. For anyone with a more scientific approach, or logical viewpoint, we may also use the term "quantum field of awareness" if that wording better suits your sensibilities.

This "God consciousness," or quantum field of awareness, exists within each of us, the code of creation exists within each of us. We have the capabilities of tapping into this infinite wisdom right now. The practice of meditation is more than most might think. It is a practice used to achieve ultimate surrender, awareness, connection, and peace of mind. Meditation does not belong to one religion or discipline. It is universal. Meditation is a doorway to a slew of things we will cover down the road. Meditation has many capabilities, but for now we will focus on it as the doorway to higher perception and awareness. Most people quit their practice, or do not commit time each and every day, so they do not experience the true depth of what is possible. Many of us have gotten complacent with external leaders or saviors coming to do the work for us, allowing us to shirk our accountability and not put the necessary time and effort into our personal and collective advancement. I will never say the truth is easy to face. It is not, and it may never be. Yet it is still the truth nonetheless, and it is the truth that will set us free. The pain of the truth forges us into who we must become, or it might be better to say: the pain of the truth inevitably brings us home to our true selves. The irrefutable truth forces us out of mental slumber and brings us into aligned action.

The difference between ultimate truth and what we are seeing play out in society today is that ultimate truth is divinely guided, a way of existing transcending all human constructs and limitations. It is the guidance of God. Everything else we are seeing play out is guided only by human ego, the need to be right, the need for more, endlessly chasing, hopelessly depending on the external as a source of fulfillment, never understanding that the key to heaven on earth is, and always has been, within us this entire time.

There is a native story, or proverb if you will, on the point of inner treasure that speaks of the hidden key to life that exists within us. It is the tale of one day when the Great spirit comes to earth with a problem. Spirit asks all the animals where to hide the great treasure of life. The first animal suggests to bury it within the earth.

Great spirit says, "No, man will dig into the earth and they will find it."

The second animal suggests it should be kept above the earth, within the stars.

Great spirit says, "No, man will even make it to the stars."

The third animal says to Great spirit, "You must send it to the depths of the seas!"

Great spirit again says, "No, man will explore the great depths of the seas as well, and they will find it there too."

The last animal, the wisest, suggests to Great spirit, "You must hide it within the hearts of themselves."

Great spirit replies, "It is done."

The key takeaway here is that through all of the external focus we have as humans, all of the achievements we have as collective, all of the triumphs, all of the exploration of our world and our galaxy, we have yet to look at the closest place to us: the inside of our own hearts. It is written in the gospel of Thomas that Jesus said, "The kingdom of heaven is spread across the earth, but men do not see it." Again, here there is the same message as in the native story: we have access to the kingdom of heaven right now.

If we could only learn to turn our eyes inward instead of being constantly externally focused. Then we would know the great mystery, we would learn how to live in peace and unity as a collective, transcending all division and corruption, and we would know the truth of our individual and collective divinity.

There is much to learn, there is much to face about the truth of our reality if we are to awaken a beautiful and sacred way of existence. This is not the fast path; this is most certainly not the easy path. It shall be spoken now: the long path and the difficult path is the most rewarding path. The greatest treasures are buried the deepest. This is why it is the long path that must be embarked on if one wishes to reap the greatest that life has to offer. There is a shedding of the layers of unconsciousness that we must leave behind. There are countless limiting beliefs that we must drop. As a serpent grows, it sheds its skin; so too must we shed the dead and old ways of existing if we are to become a new and beautiful collective. We must understand and leave our corrupted filters that have distorted how we view existence behind.

II

Filters

If you are wearing green-lensed glasses, are you seeing the natural color of the sky? If you go swimming with red-tinted goggles, are you seeing the true color of the water? It's easy to see that you are not. You are experiencing those things through a distorted lens or filter. If we are to gaze upon the majesty of truth, we must begin to understand and transcend our filters. Just as these examples are filters that distort our perception of reality, there are many other kinds of filters that greatly distort our perception of reality as well. These are much more subtle filters, so naturally, they are more difficult to become aware of. These are the filters of the mind. Since our time as infants, and even before our birth, traumatic situations and experiences have created filters in our subconscious mind, through which we have learned to navigate and judge our subjective experience of physical reality.

I attempt to convey this message with deep compassion for all who read this. These truths can be hard to hear, let alone accept. Until we go within ourselves and connect with our true divine nature, in turn bringing healing to our traumatized selves, we will continue to go through and judge life and all its happenings through the distortion of our own unconscious and unseen filters. To put it plainly, if you are alive, you have work to do on yourself. Even the most spiritually enlightened master has great internal work still to be done. One of the great missions of this beautiful physical life is to awaken deep self-awareness and self-knowledge beyond all material limitation, to shed all filters and conditioning so that only the pure essence of the true self remains.

Back to our original question: Who are you? What is left after everything you thought was you is left behind? What do you feel? How do you carry yourself in life after this reemergence of your true self? The answers to these questions will be found only by those who are courageous enough to face themselves in their entirety, those brave enough to take the accountability, to make the change, to leave all fear of the unknown behind. The caterpillar does not truly know how its transformation into a butterfly will go; it just does it because it must. Regardless of the fact that it may be hard, or extremely uncomfortable, it must be done. So too must we be willing to experience radical change in our individual lives if we are to create change on a more massive scale.

We will make a million excuses as to why we can't or don't want to do the difficult inner work; we will procrastinate and seek stimulation instead of experiencing the slow, and sometimes uncomfortable, feeling of self-improvement. It is crucial to understand that this procrastination only delays us from experiencing the true beauty of our selves—not the limited, physical perceptions of beauty, but the limitless perception of our spiritual essence as divine beings of pure energy and creation.

The delay of alignment with our true selves and the lack of connection with our individual divinity will in turn cause a delay in the experience of connection to the divinity and unification of the collective. We cannot become an externally unified collective if we are still battling the unconscious battle of individual internal separateness. We must unify ourselves internally at the individual level, and the collective external unification will inevitably follow if the true work is being done by the individual. We must leave the old ways of life behind if we are to become anew, just as the caterpillar leaves its old self behind to experience what it knows to be the next step of life. Leave all fear and excuses behind. The ego seeks to remain in comfort and therefore in control of the experience. We put the ego in check by routinely venturing beyond our comfort zone. Experiences led by the ego only lead to eventual destruction as we see all around us in this day and age. We must surrender the ego and become in alignment with the will of our soul. We must mourn ourselves deeply and fully, as we leave our old selves behind, in order to make room for what must exist in their place.

So what can we begin doing on an individual level to begin to see beyond our filters and conditioning? First, you must only accept that you have been living life through an unconscious filter, living a way that others expect you to live, or a way that even you expect yourself to live. Accepting this fact will be anything but simple; it may very well be the hardest part of this whole process. Concurrently, however, it will be the very thing that opens the doorway to infinity for you. Accepting the truth is the first step we all must take in order for deep change to begin manifesting in our society. After we accept truth, where does that leave us? After we begin to accept that the life we have been living may not be who we inherently are, what then? The very seeking of the answers to these questions is still an aspect of the ego and thinking mind. Do not seek an answer with the thinking mind; only exist as you are. Allow yourself to exist in silence or stillness, in a state of infancy, a state of rebirth if you will, a state of meditation. The meditative or transcendental state will inevitably take us to the depth of the soul.

Beyond the limitations of the ego or the limited self, we begin to understand and remember who we inherently have been this entire time. Just as the wilderness of nature goes through periods of death and rebirth with the changing of the seasons, we must also adhere to this cyclical path of death and rebirth. After all, at our core, each of us is a being of nature. We must each on our own begin a journey of transcendence, and only after beginning the transcendental journey will we realize that we always were so much more than this physical vessel or limited self. We only lost touch with the rest of our true nature. As we venture on, our next discussion will be on the transcendental and meditative practice and on the reasonings and understanding as to why it is crucial to our experience.

III

Transcendence

When you come across the words "peace" or "bliss," "purity" or "divine," "majestic" or "infinite," what comes to mind? The truth of the matter is that we all might imagine something totally different from what our peers imagine. At some point, however, we may come to a similar consensus that these terms describe some heavenly place. So if these terms are used to describe heaven, or some similar place, does that mean we can't experience these things until we "die" and go to heaven? The answer to this is quite simple. Heaven is not a place that is "there" and "then." Heaven is here and now. Again, we are brought back to the gospel of Thomas. Jesus says that the kingdom of heaven is spread across the earth, but men do not see it. Some may say this is outlandish! How can heaven be spread across this forsaken place? Surely some understand what he means here. So how is heaven spread across the earth and why don't we see it?

To put it quite simply, the reason most do not perceive the majesty of heaven is that there is still a heavy attachment to the happenings of third dimensional or physical reality. We must understand that we are beings that exist at this time with more than a physical form. We exist with a consciousness, a spirit, a soul. For those of a more logical orientation, we may refer to the spirit or the soul as the non-local self. Understand that these divine levels of ourselves (consciousness, spirit, soul) currently exist in the deeper dimensions of reality or "heaven" right now infinitely and eternally. Our blindness comes from the mega enslavement that we inflict upon ourselves in the seemingly endless chase of money, fulfillment, and pleasure. We must only begin learning practices of transcendence to spark the reawakening of the connection to our divine selves or our spiritual essence. Jesus hints here with this verse at that we are essentially "blind" to the kingdom of heaven, because the kingdom of heaven is not of a physical meaning. It can be found to be obvious that of course humans can not see the truth of heaven when heaven is primarily non physical, and all humans do is pay attention to the physical. There are many aspects of ourselves that can guide us to the truth of our current divine status and awareness; however, those are the parts of us that have been conditioned out or numbed into silence and obedience to fit into these boxes we have constructed for ourselves in this society. "Heaven" is of a deeper spiritual meaning, one that is not far or separate from who and what we are now. So to put all of the pieces together, if heaven is of a somewhat metaphysical meaning, and we live in a society where we have all but abandoned our spiritual knowledge and connection, could this be the cause of our "blindness" and cessation from heaven? To be a being of a multi-dimensional nature, or to exist with a physical and non-physical form simultaneously, and to pay attention only to the smaller, more limited portion of yourself is the same as owning a five-hundred-foot yacht and hanging out in and paying attention only to the same fifty feet of it your entire life—essentially wasting millions of dollars and wasting space that you don't even know you have to make use of, and to explore.

So far through this compilation of thought, I have expressed the importance of a meditative practice as a doorway to higher awareness.

This is not a practice reserved for those of Eastern disciplines, nor is it simply a practice to achieve peace of mind. In fact, meditation is no practice at all. Meditation is the art of non-doing. If you are consciously trying to clear your mind, or forcibly trying to rid yourself of thought, you are not in meditation. True meditation is the doorway to the rest of your awareness and perception. For humans, it is very normal for thoughts to be in our awareness. We must not force our thoughts out when we have them; we must only accept them and simply hold the door open for them to leave at their own pace. Just as if you spun the wheel of a bike or skateboard while it was suspended by a bar, eventually the wheel will stop spinning on its own. Our mind is the same; we must allow the wheel of the mind to stop spinning on its own. Simply being the observer to your thoughts will offer you a deeper state of awareness in time. We are simply observing, not interacting with our thoughts, as you might observe a bag blowing in the wind—it is as simple as this. Even if it is a pleasant thought, pay it no attention. Meditation is a non-dual state—not necessarily positive or negative, simply awareness. True meditation may also be described as accessing levels of your higher self, your spiritual essence, your divine authority, even your divine spark—the divine spark of God. When we exist in deep meditation, we must allow the entirety of our perceived physical identity to be totally and fully absorbed by our spiritual or divine spark, just as water may be fully absorbed into a towel. This in turn allows us to exist in a state of pure energetic awareness.

The state of no-self is when we begin to experience states of heaven, or heavenly awareness. The terms we used at the beginning of this chapter all begin to merge into one absolute. This happens in such a way that you begin to understand, without being told, that you have begun to scratch the surface of your divine nature.

We devote ourselves to outwardly to external religions and preachers, we pray to things outside of ourselves, and we look around outward again to find God. We look and wait with vigilance for the coming of Christ, but God has always been abundantly inside the warmth of our own hearts. The frequency of God has never left us; we are that frequency! It was only us who left ourselves. It seems the structures of the very religions put in place to help find the divine have been pointing us in the opposite direction this whole time. Look at the silliness!

In the beginning phases of developing a meditative practice, the meditation itself is not the difficulty. The difficulty comes in bringing yourself each day to your meditative practice.

Devoting the time each day is where the discipline comes in to play. This difficulty does not last, however. As you begin to experience your true divine essence, beyond the physical senses, when you begin to develop deeper perception and awareness, you then become a novice, you become absorbed into the meditative state, and there is no you left—it has become you. At times there may be potential difficulties when starting this path. Now, in respect to returning to your practice, this one is severely lessened.

Why is it difficult for us to tap into the divine state or meditative state at all? After all, we are spiritual beings. We should always have easy access to these states by this logic. It's our divine right, isn't it? Why is there a need for us to do any self-development at all?

The simplest way of answering this is to understand that religion has been playing a great prank on us. Religion tells us to look outward for God, to the skies, and await the return of the various saviors. They tell us to run door-to-door speaking of the imminent return of the divine. Religion has perfected the subtle skill of keeping us from looking inward. God has always been playing a game of divine whack-a-mole with us, and we are the moles. God is trying to connect with us, but we are in a constant state of running away from God, and we don't even know it. You must only think about it: if God and the divine are within us, and religion teaches us to look outward, take outward action, and outward study, there lies the foundation of our constant running away! We have created a sort of unconscious shield, to hide ourselves from God, and yet we tell ourselves we are seekers of God. This is why the meditative state is difficult to access for humans.

What is happening in true states of meditation is essentially the coming home to our selves with our tails between our legs in complete surrender. I mention surrender here because this is the point at which we begin to understand that it is now time to surrender our shields that we have put up against God and allow the truth of what God is to be known to us, individually, through direct experience of the divine through various spiritual practices.

The fact that what we have been trying is not working begins to become clear to us now, and that realization holds us with compassion as we cry and mourn and create space for our true ways of being to come fourth. It creates a satisfying and fantastical smile and sigh of relief when you begin to realize that the finding of God does not actually involve any searching at all! We must only sit and allow God to become known to us; we must only know that God has been sitting at the table next to us this entire time, simply waiting for us to look over and realize we are one and the same.

All of this running around tirelessly, doing what the clergyman or preacher says, listening to all of the wonderful stories of Christ or Mohammad coming to save us, when we don't really have to do much besides wait, are now seeming all the more foolish. Christ never left us; it was in fact we who left him. Christ consciousness has always been available to us if we only choose to allow it to be. The journey of transcendence actually involves very little action at all.

It is simply the letting go of who and what we thought we were, based on what we were taught we must do and how we must act in society based upon foundations and beliefs passed down for generations. It is time to ask yourself, are you ready to finally break the unconscious contract of subconscious conditioning? Are you ready to finally be you? Next, we will break through the fear of change, allowing us to take the necessary steps to find out who we are.

IV

Fear of change

A disclaimer: this section may be very triggering to some. Many things are brought up here that we may not be taking the necessary time to look at or think about. It is not my intention here to stir anger, but there are certain things that must be said, so we shall discuss them here. The purpose of this section is to simply bring awareness to our fear of change. Change is not always comfortable; therefore this section will not always feel comfortable, especially for those who have been consistently turning a blind eye toward truth. There is a deep reason for all that is shared here, and it will tie into all that we have been discussing. With that being said, let us begin.

If a young boy is drowning, and you have the necessary skills to save him, would you? Now, we can expect that most people if confronted with this situation would not hesitate to save the child. Of course though, everything is easy when it is a hypothetical. If I am a good swimmer and a child is drowning, I will jump into the water and save the child no matter whose child it is, because it is the positive thing to do, on the moral basis of compassion for all life. Simple.

Let's take that same perspective to society. It is quite simple to look outside at the world and see that the state of things are at an all-time low. You might even say the world is "drowning." We are all aware of this feeling in the world today. We are aware that all of our politicians are corrupt, likely having taken or given bribes to get ahead at some point in their career. Regardless of what "side" you believe you are on, or what your belief system is, these points remain true.

It is insanity that we have this awareness of corruption in our system yet we still vote the same people into office year after year. Why do we do this? We must ask ourselves this question. Maybe we consciously turn our minds away from the blatant corruption because we think ourselves small and we have no clue what we can do about it, if anything. Maybe we are afraid that our "friends" will no longer accept us if we stand for what we believe is right. Maybe we've been following the herd for so long that we've subconsciously given up any hope for change and just accepted that this is the way things are now. Religion has made us submissive in this way. For eons, we've been told—and we've believed—that some Christ-like savior will come and rescue us from damnation and suffering. What a wonderful story indeed. As we sit here waiting for that great prophecy to be fulfilled, as we sit here waiting for that ultimate promise to be kept, all of the children are effectively drowning, and we have been conditioned to do nothing about it. Is it not our responsibility? We already established that we would save the child even if they weren't our own.

When a hypothetical becomes non-hypothetical, it isn't so easy of a choice. How many corrupt leaders will we continue electing? How many unanswered prayers will be sent? How much more child trafficking must happen? How many more genocides must take place before we dust off our boots, tighten our laces, and take the necessary steps to bring peaceful and loving change to our world? A question: if there were a vending machine that you know is broken, would you keep putting your money into it hoping it would eventually magically start working and give you what you want? Or would you go find

FEAR OF CHANGE

another vending machine that actually works? Most likely you would find a new machine. This is an analogy to our current system; we keep investing our time and money into this system, but nothing changes. We must stop putting our money into a broken vending machine.

We live in a society where those with parental responsibilities satisfy themselves and their egos by saying they don't have the time to work on themselves, or to make a change in their lives, or talk about something that could be seen as controversial. They say they need to maintain a "real" job to provide for their children. "Providing for your children" is an interesting phrase. What is better for your children than providing them with a better world? We must realize and begin to accept that true change cannot and will not come without being slightly uncomfortable for a time. If you want something new, you must do something new. It cannot be made simpler than this. We cannot be afraid of losing the Maya, or illusion of ourselves; we must have no fear of being rejected by our social circles if we embark on a journey of growth. We have the most what we might call "friends" when we are at our lowest times because a part of us is unfulfilled, so we surround ourselves with others to help us stay away from looking at ourselves. This is one of the many reasons we have the saying "misery loves company." If we are to every truly meet the divine, we must not fear losing ourselves.

We say we want the guidance of God, we love to say God is good, and yet we keep detaching ourselves from God, and we replace our divine union with cheap pleasure and stimulation. We hopelessly try to create our own rules and expectations from a logical perspective. If we want to live in true alignment with divine energy and guidance, we must surrender all attempts to control the happenings of this life. We must surrender all fear of facing the depths of the unknown and all of its vastness. We must surrender the desire of seeking pleasure and comfort over facing the truth that surrounds us. When the resistance to truth is dropped, and we truly surrender our ego and the need to be correct, then the true essence and divine majesty of God becomes powerfully observable in our lives. These greatest of treasures require time and devotion, they require change, they require us putting our status down and taking accountability for our world, and ourselves. We must not allow our conditioned minds to limit us from the perception and wisdom of what is truly possible. If we only allow ourselves to live with an open mind, to live without fear, to be truly open to learning and experiencing the divinity of this existence, then we will unify and rejoice in the hidden heaven that is spread across the earth.

Just imagine that for a moment: a unified world, a world of fairness and equality, far from greed and corruption, war, and suffering. It is beautiful to imagine, isn't it? We must come back to the understanding that if we are to unify our world, we must transcend this system that is fundamentally based on separation: left vs. right, black vs. white, this religion vs. that religion, this party vs. that party, this country vs. that country.

A system that is fundamentally based on sides and parties such as these cannot be used as a blueprint for unification, as I have repeatedly said throughout these pages. This is a very hard and uncomfortable truth, knowing that our past ways of leading life cannot fundamentally work or support the desired level of existence that we imagine having. Simply accepting this truth is the first step to awakening. Do not fear or worry about what will come next, or how we will move forward; the code for existing in divine alignment with each other and our environment exists within us. If you wish to know how to move forward, or what to expect next, all answers to all situations can be found in the depths of your own soul. Change is inevitable; whether we would have it or not, it is coming. The thing about change however, is that it is infinitely easier to go through when it is accepted and flowed with. It is much easier to flow with change than resist it. Sure, at first it is not easy. We only must allow ourselves to humbly come before the universe, surrendering all control and expectation, and then the universe guides you into the flow states of being. Resisting change and clinging or clutching to familiarity is the root cause of all suffering. This concept of clinging and attachment as the root of all suffering is spoken of in the four noble truths of Buddhism. In brief summary, the four noble truths teach about the clinging and clutching to things in life as the root cause of all suffering. We must release this attachment to transient things, and move with the ever changing flow of existence. We create our own suffering by attaching ourselves to a myriad of things.

This can be an attachment to your belief system, to your relationships, even to your money and other material things. The reason this clinging or attaching to things causes suffering is first that they are transient, meaning they are impermanent. They have the capability of leaving or changing. So when something happens to these things that we have idolized, we feel as if we've lost a part of ourselves, because we clutched on too tightly, and now it has left. We have allowed these things to become us, to take over our identity and sense of self, even to the point now at which we don't know who we are without these things we attach ourselves to. We have effectively lost ourselves. Through this loss of connection to our true selves we have begun, and chosen the way, of misaligned action. Even though this misaligned action may bring a sense of fulfillment for a time, it will be limited. There is no deep spiritual bond to these external things, (money, houses, cars, sexual partners, etc.) so they stagnate in time. Let's say, that you have achieved what you believe in your own way to be "ultimate fulfillment"; you've acquired what you think you need and want. You've got the money and the house, but how long until you desire a new house or more money? Or a faster car? Or newer car? Desire at the surface level always demands more in order to create contentment there is never slowness or ease. Lets say that even through this you insist that these things bring you great joy and that everything is well and good.

Is it really? How long can an individual's contentment last before he begins to feel uneasy turning a blind eye to the rest of the suffering around this place we call home? Now understand, I do not say this to demand others give up what they have earned; I say this simply to point to the knowledge that even observable success does not mean you are living in alignment with the positive divine code of creation. Example: A corporation makes billions of dollars by cutting down and destroying nature, but they are now considered monetarily successful. This is a dramatic example, but that does not make it any less true. The corporation is rich and successful beyond measure, but they acquired wealth in a way out of alignment with the divine source. We all must inspect our lives and look to see where we are living out of divine alignment. In modern society, we have been led to believe that after we achieve external fulfillment, we will feel internally fulfilled as well. This could not be further from the truth. The hermetic principle that many are familiar with, "as within so without," will explain how this is false. What is meant here, simply put, is that our external reality is a mirror of our internal reality. This can easily be verified by looking around at our world today. A majority of humans live life without the smallest hint of a spiritual discipline, and beings that are of spirit and have no spiritual discipline is a formula for annihilation. We do not practice an internal discipline, and our society is in ruins, a state of deterioration. It is plain to see, but for many, it will be hard to accept. Again, a point that can be taken from this chapter is simply that we must accept change, we must not fear change, and change is on our doorstep whether we accept it or not. Do not fear the consequences of change.

Only have faith that there is an inherent plan, benevolent to all life and all creation that is encoded into our very DNA—a code that we can access through spiritual discipline.

"People don't realize how hard it is to speak the truth to a world full of people that don't realize they are living a lie." —Edward Snowden

V

The Great Act

"All the world's a stage, and all the men and women merely players."
—William Shakespeare

Just as the foot may wear many myriads of socks and shoes, the foot remains the same. Just as a hand may put on many different gloves, the hand remains the same. Just as a snake wears many skins over a lifetime, the inherent nature of the snake does not change. We too as humans must understand that beyond these sleeves of mortality lies our true nature: a nature of divinity, a nature of majesty, a nature of eternity. It is important to know this and be aware of this because if we continue to identify with and perpetuate the attachment to the lowest aspects of ourselves, which is the physical self, then for a time, our inherent divine essence or our true nature will be dimmed.

We will then continue to seek answers from old, dying, and outdated systems because we are still unconscious of our true nature. Just as the laws and theories of science evolve with time, so too must the way we govern and lead our lives. If evolution of these points does not occur, we will continue to reap what we are currently sowing, which is the misalignment of the mind, body, and spirit at the individual level, which creates misalignment at the collective level. We must transcend this subtle act that we are all a part of and have been part of since beginningless time. The soul, the consciousness, the spirit, may possess many physical forms; it is merely a force of cosmic energy dancing as a beautifully imperfect being of physicality for a short time. The problem lies in the understanding that we have forgotten that we are the cosmic energy that is simply using a body and we now believe that we are the physical form, or this ego construct. Through the meditative discipline, we shall begin to deepen our awareness and begin to remember that we are in fact, not this body, but eternal, limitless, formless energy that for a time is experimenting with the limited nature of the formed or third dimension. We rush around, day to day, as if there is something massive and of utmost importance that we must achieve here. We collect money and material things, and we grow old and we tell ourselves that we've done it. We've finished. What have you really done? What have you really finished? Do we really know? Are we capable of knowing?

All of this rushing around from this to that, from pleasure to pleasure, stimulation to more stimulation, causes our lives to fly by, seemingly out of our hands. The most apparent evidence of this is the common phrase "life is short." In truth, life is very long; it is only perceived as short because modern humans have forgotten how to remain present. They exist with divided attention, so naturally life seems to have hastened or shortened. It is only their mind that has become fractured or divided trying to juggle ten things at once. So we see that life isn't actually short; it is the human mind and attention that has become divided, causing life to seem short, because full awareness of the present moment has been taken away.

Here is an example. If I ask you to focus on a pencil with your nearly full attention, it's a fairly easy task, and the pencil seems full and large and detailed. Now, if I ask you to remain focused on the pencil, but now I ask you to complete five other tasks while focusing on the pencil still, the pencil now seems smaller because your mind is fractured trying to do many other things now. So you see, in this way we view life as being short, but it is we who have become short with our attention to the present. We have forgotten how to remain still, to be fully here and now, in the present moment. Many humans have a shared experience of what we know as depression. A simple way that we may tie in depression with this line of thought is that depression is a war between the spirit and the conscious mind. Our spirit or soul is tapped into the divine at all times; however, our conscious mind is influenced immensely by our waking reality. This includes our traumas, our conditionings, our upbringings, and the influence of religious structures we may have had early in life, all of the way into adulthood. So because of these things that have conditioned our minds to behave in such a way, we currently choose, consciously or not, to act against the will of our soul with the belief that we know what is best. This may feel fine or acceptable for a time, but when the soul pulls in one direction and we resist like a dog pulling and resisting on a leash in another direction, this creates two opposing forces within us. This internal war manifests externally as feelings of being lost or unmotivated for anything in life. We are caught in this internal war, not knowing which way to go or what to do; we know this as depression.

This is why we must emphasize the importance of allowing the soul to guide us. To allow the soul to guide us is to allow the divine to guide us. It is uncomfortable at first, but that is only because we are not used to being led by the soul. We have instead allowed our egos, fears, and subjective beliefs to guide our lives. Someone who spends their entire life in darkness or Maya will obviously be resistant to light and truth at the beginning. Through the continuous attempts of the exploration of the self, and the continuous release of clutching tightly to attachments through meditation, accepting the divine truth becomes as easy and nourishing as drinking a cup of water. We are, by design, made to be drinking this "divine water," but we have been sold poison for so long that poison has become our water, and even darker, we believe that this poison is our water. This is the great act, because upon embarking on a journey of true self-knowledge, one realizes "neti neti," which is Sanskrit for "not this, not that." One loses one's subjugation to the restriction of physical reality. In other words, one realizes one's true God nature. As with all learning and growth, this understanding will come in time, and is not too necessary to be fully focused on now. We are not this body, and not that body; we are each of us the eternal all. The analogy of the diamond is best to represent this idea.

There are many facets to a diamond that are, for the most part, of equal size and power as the facets next to them—no more, no less. So, in this same way, there are many individual perspectives to our physical reality that are just as real, vivid, and as strong as our own. This is key to grasp, because this will help us awaken deeper compassion for all humans, because we will learn to understand and accept the fact that others have their way of thinking based on their own internal systems just as we do. We need not force our beliefs on others; we must instead learn to understand their perspectives by asking questions and inquiring as to why they think how they think. This allows us to understand others we disagree with on a deeper level, and then find a place of common ground that we may build upon, while still having our differences. So if all perspectives are essentially equally powerful and vivid, whose ideas or perspectives do we listen to? The Zen master will tell you to listen to none. Each facet of the diamond merely holds its own perspective, subjective view, or portion of truth. No single facet contains the entire truth. Even partial collections of facets or groups still do not hold the entire truth.

"The Perennial Philosophy," by Aldous Huxley, speaks of the inherent or total truth of reality. This is the inherent truth that all religions or spiritual disciplines try to point toward in their own way. Christianity speaks of heaven; Eastern traditions speak of enlightenment, nirvana, moksha, or samadhi. In their essence, they speak of the same thing. The limitations of human language lessens the portrayal of divine truth. This divine truth has only been changed and adapted according to specific traditions, cultural differences, and geographical locations where ancient teachings are found. We again only want to believe that our religion or path is correct, because we still operate from a place of ego and non-awareness. Divine truth cannot be fully expressed through modern religion. It is an impossible task. We must understand that total truth is limitless and cannot be fully expressed or known through usual human concepts. So to try to create rules, regulations, and systems to be followed is already out of alignment with the divine because we are trying to create rules and systems for something that is not and cannot be fully understood by humans. Go try to fit the entire ocean into a cup from your cabinet and see how well it works. This again points us back to the fact that religion is something that holds humanity back from soul-level evolution. There is no single religion or path that is correct. No single facet carries the higher perspective of total truth, no matter how hard it tries. Concurrently, however, there is no religion or path that is wrong. All paths and religions are still a form of ego and separation. When we identify with one group or another, we have put an unconscious barrier up to all other groups that are "different" from our group, thus furthering our separation within the collective. Different religions and groups must be transcended and let go of for a deeper sense of unification to manifest. When deeper unification occurs within the collective, it allows room for a single, divine, and inherent truth to begin coming to fruition in our society.

My point within these pages is not to convert you or sell you some new age idea; I only attempt to provide a deeper perspective, and to inspire the seeking mind that lives within each of us to question everything we think we know, to brave the depths of the vastness of the unknown. The heaven that we seek as humans is already within the palm of our hands, we only have yet to look. The true divinity and true nature of our spiritual essence is not something that is on hold until we "die." It is something that is meant to be known and experienced here and now while still in the heat of this physical experience. We are, by definition, spiritual beings—it is a fact that we have a spirit and consciousness—therefore, it seems silly to state that our spiritual essence is reserved to be experienced at some later time. This "spirit" that we have, has taken many names over time. Some names are "prana" or "chi" simply meaning the energy of life. It is a part of you, perhaps the biggest part. To say your spiritual knowledge is on hold is the same as saying your arm is on hold for a later time. Your arm is a part of you just as your spirit or soul is a part of you. Just the fact that we have lost connection to our true essence does not mean that it is not there.

The spirit and soul simply exist in a deeper dimension in the reality of the self. We are beings of a multi-dimensional nature, and we infinitely have access to the fullness of our multi-dimensional selves. We only exist in a society that has grown cut off from spirit in almost all ways. In society, it is almost seen as taboo when someone speaks about higher awareness. Actually, it is how we are made to be. The hard truth here is that we have become hopelessly asleep to our true nature because of the many conditionings and cheap comforts of modern time.

Our personal traumas and individual hardships have caused us to turn our eyes away from our internal selves, because it is uncomfortable to face these things. When we turn our eyes away from our internal reality, we also turn our eyes away from our higher awareness, our connection to the divine, and our true selves. We currently exist in a society based on ego and power, and that is exactly why we feel that these deeper truths are of a foreign nature. Ego is very shallow, surface-level. So when we exist with a shallow society for so long, of course anything with true depth will seem uncomfortable and unnatural. These deeper truths, however, are the very things that shape our reality. We have allowed fear to take hold of us, we have allowed fear to take over our minds and our will. We fear not having enough money, enough food, enough energy, enough love, enough shelter, the list goes on and on. Our fear and our attachment to material things has made us easy to control. We have become dependent on the external world as well as physical things. Our clutching causes our suffering.

We clutch to our beliefs and our desires because we do not realize this physical world is Maya, the great illusion. We have no internal foundation or cultivation, and this makes us all slaves to the outside world. We must awaken from this deep slumber; we must remember our truth as individuals and then as a collective. We must shed and let go of all fear, transcend all conditioning of the external, and exist as purified and sovereign awareness. This is the point (if we can even say such a thing) of meditation. In true states of meditation, the thing that happens is the cessation of the meditator. One is no more. Full merging with the divine has taken place. Upon this point, one realizes total fulfillment, total bliss of the highest order. Meditation is merely the portal or gateway between physical awareness and higher awareness. Connection to the infinitely divine aspects of reality become powerfully vivid to the meditator who has become absorbed by the divine spark. This, unfortunately, cannot be perfectly described with the use of language. This can only be experienced, and then understood. This divine realization causes all unnecessary attachment to the physical to fall away. When the divine is re-realized by the self, the physicality of this third dimension begins to have a meek feeling, it begins to not be sufficient enough anymore.

This happens because the seeker has now begun to experience the true essence of his divine nature. Now, when we experience the true mystical happenings of infinite reality on a mass scale as a collective, our society will have no choice but to adapt and change with us. When we are no longer pleased by physical things alone, those who benefit from our attachment to physical things lose their power and control over society, because certain goods and services will no longer be of interest to the public. Such groups as corrupt corporations and politicians will lose the immense power that they currently have because there is no longer a need for their corrupt and poisonous services when the divine is realized. So, this will cause corrupt establishments and groups to severely change how they operate, including new rules and regulations that benefit all, or they will be made to give up their positions and fall into the background of the story, because the awakening of humanity will have begun. The common people will begin to see the silliness of their own attachments and no longer support big businesses or give their time, energy, and money to old systems, or old unconscious ways of existence. Thus, heaven on earth will begin to not seem so far away. If we wish for a heavenly place on earth, we must allow the divine to guide us there. Only the divine has the blueprint and the wisdom to bring fourth the world we seek. Not our elected leaders. We must each of us go within and touch the divine, which in turn will create a divine space large enough to plant the seeds and awaken the foundation for true heaven on earth.

VI
Opening the Heart to Truth

If a man has spent fifty years inside of a tiny box, and he had complete freedom as long as he stayed inside of his box, of course he will learn to love his box. He has decorated his box, he invites others into his box, he's even gotten married and had children inside of his box. He loves his box. He has not realized that his box is the very prison that keeps him unconscious of reality. It is a prison, though, that is of genius design. These are the mental prisons that we have unconsciously created for ourselves. So we are not capable of realizing that we are in fact, inside of prisons of our own making until we do the necessary inner work. The concept of these prisons was not made by us, but we are the ones who have adopted them and perpetuated them for millennia. We have divided ourselves into groups with those whose prisons are similar to ours in some way. These can be religious identification, political affiliation, skin color, music taste, class or status—the list is unending. Yet as hard as people work to strengthen their identities, the further they get from who they really are. We have been subtly influenced to separate ourselves based on these ideas, through subconscious programming, to such an extent that we have forgotten we are one race of people.

We look outward to small external leaders, when we could be turning our eyes inward to the true essence and majesty of God that is within each of us. We have only to decide that we are one people, and that we are united, rather than hoard our riches for the advancement of "our side." Men with power only want one thing: more power. When people stand together, these men know that their power and control become in jeopardy of being taken away from them, and therein lies the reason for the multitude of systems that create the perpetual illusion of separation among our kind. There are those who benefit from our separation and unconsciousness, so there are measures in place to make us believe we are separate from our fellow humans. We must accept that we have done the damnedest things, we must accept that we have all been wrong, we must drop the stories of old that have been given to us by those in power, we must each of us look at the world through the eyes of a newborn. We must close our eyes to the stories and gab of the outside; we must open our inner eye and allow God to become known. This in a way is what Einstein meant with his famous quote. To achieve new results, we must take new action. It will be hard, it will be uncomfortable, but we must change. The outside world can only change after we have done the necessary work internally. External reality is a mirror of internal reality. The hermetic principle "as above so below, as within so without, as the universe so the soul" shows this to be true. The level of alignment that we achieve as a collective internally will be reflected by the status of the advancement of our external collective. A poorly aligned internal system will create a poor and crumbling world. A strong and affirmed internal system will manifest outwardly as a flourishing society. Coincidence? You decide. The only obstacle we now face as a society is the fear of jumping off the edge into the unknown. We fear the change, and we fear the work that comes with change. We fear that if we jump, we may not be caught. The truth is that we are our own saviors. If you fear not being caught, just remember that you are the divine, and the only one with this fear is you. Know that you are eternally and divinely guided.

Know that you are inherently abundant and blissful beyond what the physical world might be showing you. Simply opening your heart to the infinite possibilities and potentials of the unknown is all that is required as the first step to a more divine or higher understanding of ourselves and our reality. Do not fear starting over. The earth goes through seasons of change, periods of death and rebirth, so we as humans must also follow this divine flow of change that is life. Our suffering comes from when we resist change, when we try to resist what is happening, because we think that we can control what might happen. If you are in a pool and you are constantly complaining and splashing around, moving around, what happens? The water ripples and moves away from you. When you are completely still while in water, what happens? The water is able to come toward you. If you truly seek deeper divine connection and awareness, you must be still, you must be at peace with what is. When you are in states of deep stillness, you do not need to seek the divine. When you are truly still and ready, the divine will come to you.

It cannot be stressed any more at this point that until we truly learn to open our hearts to the infinity of what is truly possible, we will indefinitely remain in these same patterns. We are worth heaven on earth; the reason we do not experience heaven on earth is that we are divided. God is waiting for us to remember and learn of our own divinity and unite ourselves before the realm of majesty is readily and easily available to all. There are countless of those who have already experienced the mystical and divine nature of life to certain extents—we may know them as gurus, mystics, wisdom keepers, philosophers, divinely inspired poets and artists—and who are ready to share their findings with the world. We must only learn to surrender our ego and say that we are ready for a change. When the student is ready, the teacher will appear. If there is no room in the student's cup, there is no room for the teacher to share or impart wisdom. Not until we can become comfortable, and slowly learn to accept the possibility that we have been hopelessly confused for millennia, can we begin to empty and make room in our cup. To look at the current trend of our world, and to say that things are sane or working properly is insanity. If we believe that our cup is full, then advancing as a society beyond this current state is an impossibility because we tell ourselves that we already know the best way. Or we tell ourselves that we are good at making all decisions in divinely just ways. There is no interest in change with this mindset, so aligned change can never come. The equation, again, is quite simple and plain to see. The continuation of old rules and regulations will continue to reap more of the same old struggle that we already know. New patterns and new ways of being will create new results and a new sense of a just existence. Beginning the path of change is never easy, we don't always know where to begin. So, that is what we will discuss next: developing the beginner's path.

VII

Developing the Beginner's Path

Many who hear the phrase "making a radical change in life" think that it means they will lose certain things that they enjoy in life. Due to this fear of loss, we close our eyes to change, and in turn we close our eyes to our potential. The mission here is to simply dispel that fear. It is far from the truth to think that radical change means losing all that we enjoy from life. I do not mean to mislead, so yes, certain things will be lost, but concurrently, certain things stay the same, and certain things will be gained. This is inevitable with all change. We need not worry about this now, however. Firstly, when developing a path of deeper exploration into life, an honest assessment of our individual life is necessary. A simple observation of our habits, routines, and lifestyle choices is needed so we can see where our time is going and how efficiently we are spending it. We all have the time to implement new ways of being, but we have learned and become accustomed to prioritizing pleasure. We must be willing to sacrifice some of our pleasure in order to cultivate the true depths of our consciousness. All paths of positive change require consistent inner work.

Inviting mindfulness into our lives is key for inner work to flourish. Meditation is one of the most common practices to deepen mindful awareness. Sitting in states of purified stillness and surrender allows us to transcend our physical senses for a time, connecting back to the divine nature of our soul. As spiritual beings, we need a spiritual care routine that goes beyond normal prayer. Just as cars need maintenance, we need routine spiritual maintenance to remain in alignment with divine will. Just as with vehicles, when we ignore scheduled maintenance, things start to underperform, and eventually, they stop working entirely. The same applies to us as spiritual beings. If we neglect our spiritual selves, we become out of alignment with our soul and the divinity of existence. Each day we must have time for states of meditation. We must devote time to these parts of ourselves. The most difficult part of meditation for the beginner is simply showing up. After time spent in meditation, the divine becomes as easily visible to us as our pens and pencils.

We just have to be willing to commit to ourselves. Simply look at life, look where things can be moved and schedules can be adjusted to make time for a routine spiritual practice. Spend less time with TV, spend less time going out, etc. There is always time when we prioritize ourselves beyond the levels of pleasure. Wake up a little earlier, go to sleep a little later—there is always time. It is again a matter of priorities and the willpower to choose and commit to change. You do not need to be a Zen master sitting in meditation ten hours a day; anything as little as twenty minutes a day will suffice if that is all you can truly afford. What matters most is your intention to return to your practice every day without making excuses for yourself. If you commit to yourself, the universe will commit to you. This is how it must be. As you commit to a daily practice, it will begin to evolve on its own as you evolve and grow, reaching new levels of self-awareness and true awareness of reality. Everything you thought would be difficult has become quite simple, because you are now falling into deeper alignment with the pull of your soul. You are simply along for the ride, the vessel for a truly deep spirit. The more time we spend in meditation, the more self-aware we may become, beyond just our physical selves. Our true nature as formless beings of light, power, and majesty becomes known. The more time we spend in meditation, the deeper realizations of life we begin to have and the more we begin to experience how things should be.

I have no specific path to offer or convey here. The only non-negotiable is that we all experience the truth of the divine for ourselves, not by what we are told by others. This includes all teachers, preachers, priests, mystics, and gurus. The divine allows us to not need everyone to agree with us; the divine understanding allows us to cohesively exist in a world where we don't agree with everyone, yet society still advances, unifies, and evolves through our differences of opinion. However, it is still a world where we have unconditional love and compassion for all life here, even all who disagree with us. This is the key that will allow us to advance regardless of our differences, because we will realize a shared inner divine truth that is beyond our differences. This is why inner work and deep awareness are needed. This is the key that we are missing now. This is the beginning of awakening.

Through the routine experience of our true energetic nature in meditation, and the consistent alignment of ourselves with the flow and structure of divine creation, the bliss of unified existence begins to manifest outwardly in small ways as the noticeable positive changes and habitual upgrades of our lifestyles. We will notice how much better we feel, how much lighter we feel, how much more connected to life we feel, how much more fulfilled we feel; enlightenment is not reserved for a holy few. We are each of us equally of divine creation. We will notice that we begin to show up more fully in the world, for ourselves and others. Others notice your evolution and become inspired to incite their own awakening and growth. Through this though, we must not attach ourselves to a desired goal or outcome, because if said goal or desire is not reached, more suffering comes from this. We must only exist in the present, allowing life and our experiences to unfold as they must. Our non-attached selves allow for a deeper experience, with less suffering, because our happiness and fulfillment are not dependent on the completion of some goal. After manifestations of change have become noticeable, and a regular occurrence, these internal reflections and internal levels of healing begin to take even greater levels of manifestation. Now we begin attracting new people and experiences that are aligned with our newly awakened self. Others who mirror your path in some way will become known to you. The magnetic nature between awakening souls is stronger than any relationship we may try to force in our lives. Beyond this, we begin to see a collective shift in divine awareness. As within, so without. What happens on the inside will show on the outside. It will always be internal first, and then outward. It can never be outside first for lasting positive change. Someone who experiences trauma will not experience true healing by looking to the outside. We must look within ourselves to bring healing to the shattered parts of ourselves. The truth is that if you are alive, you have healing to do. As we commit to our paths, we must not allow the opinions of others to deter us from the great work.

Many will challenge you, many will look down on the change you are making, but this does not matter. You know why you are embarking on this journey of divine awareness and surrender. This work is not meant for those who desire quick, fast, and easy results. The natural unfolding of divine creation is of a slow and subtle nature. We must leave the speed of modern society behind and return to the true natural flow of being. Things that come easy are never substantial or long lasting. The greatest treasures are found by exploring the depths of the earth for decades and centuries, not a day or a week. This path is beautiful because each day small treasures and synchronicities are noticed, small changes find their way into our lives, when we truly let the divine lead, and the day will come when you look at your life and see the immense progress awakened in your life for the positive. When we develop a deep relationship and alignment with the true divinity of our spiritual essence and soul, literal magic takes place in life: the ancient, natural magic that was a normal experience for native cultures all around the world. This magic is our divine birthright, but we must be willing to commit to ourselves to have these experiences. It will not come otherwise. We have only chosen money over magic in these modern times.

Those closest to you may not understand this awakening part of you; they may not wish to join you or be a part of it. That is okay. Everyone is on their own timeline. When we do the personal work with integrity, strength, and commitment, the fire will spread, and your newly awakened self, your newly aligned energy, will become contagious to those around you. You may very well be the inspiration those around you have been waiting for. You will be the inspiration for them to begin or deepen their own self connection and awareness. We cannot do this work alone. You may face many things about this path seemingly alone, but that does not mean it will always be this way.

Many on this planet are being called to awaken at this time. The true divine is calling us home. The corruption, the greed, and the conflicts of our world are becoming more blatant and obvious. This will serve as a catalyst for those who are willing to hear and be accepting of a deeper truth. Our souls, our spirit guides, and the universe are nudging us now, at this time, to return to the divine truth, the divine and sacred ways of being. This is so that we may experience what a truly unified collective is like—a world that doesn't know suffering, war, poverty, and sickness. The only one in our way is us. As we deepen our spiritual and divine connection, the less ego-centered we become, the less we have the urge or need to be right, and through this, the collective shall achieve a state of advancement and unification. One person at a time. The fire is rising; whether we rise with it or burn is a choice that is left with us.

VIII

The Pathless Path

The very nature of the soul, or the divine, is limitless. There is no scripture that can fully describe the divine, and there is no single correct route of divine expression. There are no words that can fully encapsulate the divine because words are a limited concept. You cannot use mere words to convey divinity in its entirety, just as you cannot pour the entire ocean into a single cup. This is the contradiction that we are faced with in religion. We make boxes and rules, and we tell ourselves that this is how the divine works, and this is what we must do to achieve the divine. God has never existed inside of these labels and boxes we have created. We believe we know the truth after attempting to read translated scripture. Existence is constantly changing and growing. Therefore, trying to capture the true infinite happenings of the divine is a fool's errand. It is pure ego. We can never fully know the truth while in physical form because the physical cannot contain the infinite nature and truth of all that is the divine. We must do away with our trying to grasp the infinite and simply experience the divine unfoldment as it happens. This releases suffering when we learn to let go the need to label and understand all things logically. True beauty can come forth when we do not have the need or urge to box things up. All religions and disciplines point toward the one perennial philosophy. Whether you call it nirvana, heaven, samadhi, or enlightenment, it is all the same thing at the core.

We must let go of our books that we externally cling to for answers. We must turn our eyes inward to experience the very thing we have been searching for in these books. The true divine blueprint, or the perennial philosophy, exists eternally inside each of us, as I have said myriad times. Just as computer programs are the internal codes and structures for the happenings of a computer, we must only look internally within ourselves to begin learning. This inner looking, or self-knowledge, begins in states of meditation, the letting go of all control, the ultimate surrender. Only through the surrendering of the self or the ego will the divine become knowable to the seeker. Only through a giving up of the attachment to our beliefs of what might be, so that we can experience the full potential of what can be. Just as we cannot control the flow of the ocean, the ripple of divine creation cannot be fully held by any human concept. It is a certain infinite spiraling outward of consciousness that we must only align in accordance with. The ever-expanding nature of space is simply a direct mirror of the infinite reaches of the spiritual essence contained within each of us. At the same time, there is nothing to do, but there is also everything to do. The only logical step now is to give over, or surrender, all control to the divine. It's just as if you were watching a movie or film: you don't try to control the movie, you simply observe and enjoy what is happening on the screen. Such is the way we must learn to experience life: without trying to control every outcome of every situation. Alignment of a divine order will come only when we surrender our individual egos, to align with the greater flow of all creation.

This may be a very far-out or rather weird way of looking at life for many. This is simply because we have become so used to rushing, struggling, and forcing our lives to work out how we want. We can simply know that this method of society or existence cannot be in alignment with the divine because of the levels of stress that it causes in the lives of most who live this way. Something that is of true divine order will be easy, blissful, and fulfilling. This isn't to say life will be without hardship, but there will be a deeper understanding of life, and thus a deeper understanding of why we go through certain hardships. We only must allow ourselves to step back and return to the divine spark that we carry within us. It is merely because we have seemingly separated ourselves from our divinity that we believe we must be the slave drivers of our lives. This has never been true. Unfortunately, this way of being is not spoken of in mainstream media, because there are those who benefit greatly from us not being in alignment with our true nature and our true selves. Beings that are in alignment with the truth of their spiritual essence cannot be controlled or manipulated. This is the reason awakening souls are a threat to an established society. Many awakening souls are passed off as conspiracy theorists, or crazy, or mentally unstable, in an effort to keep the public masses unaware of a deeper truth. Even so, we cannot stop change from happening any more than we can stop the seasons from changing or the sun from setting. Change and awakening are an inevitable part of our existence. It is simply that we are fighting against and resisting this inevitable change. The more we resist this change, the more difficult life becomes, the more uncomfortable we become, and the more difficult change itself becomes.

A question: if something is inevitable for all life, why resist it? We can understand that the true way of experiencing life is pathless by looking at the natural flow of the elements and the energy that surrounds us and flows through us. First, we look at how water flows: there is no one forced way that water must move. It takes the path of least resistance. It takes the shape of whatever space it exists within. We are no different from this water. Our life can be as simple as flowing water, but we try so hard to control the path of our flow. It is a foolish thing to try and control the divine unfoldment of life. Bruce

Lee said it best: "Be water, my friend." This could not be a more perfect example.

The ways of peace are all around us. Peace cannot come from trying to control what might be. Do not fight the uncomfortable things in life, simply practice non-attachment; this helps us to understand our hardships rather than become stuck in a loop trying to avoid or fix them at all costs. We must understand that we are not this experience, and that this life does not define who we are. It is our reactions and responses to certain situations that define who we are. Here again we return to the the four noble truths of Buddhism. We must release ignorance and let go of the premeditated perception of how we wish for things to turn out. We must fill ourselves with divine connection, and in turn our physical attachments will lose the power they hold over our lives. We will realize that we are the source of our own fulfillment, and we will look no longer to the outside world to satisfy us. Now, this is not to say the material world is somehow negative or bad; that is not my point here. This is only to show that the control that the material realm has over us will cease. It is quite great to indulge the senses in physicality. Now we can do so with a fuller spectrum of awareness because we are not hopelessly expending effort to get something from the physical world.

The way we enjoy a play or a movie is the way we will be able to enjoy our own lives, because we are now less attached to the outcome. Therefore, less stress comes because we now understand that things change and flow beyond our control. Just as when you are watching a film, you may become sad when your favorite character suffers some unfortunate event, but then you move on with the rest of the film, and then you return to your life quite all right because you know it was only a film, and these things happen. Life is the same. Things happen, and much of the time they are beyond our control. So to put it plainly, trying to control the uncontrollable is a terrible fate for the spirit. If you asked ten different philosophers about the formation of attachment, you would get ten different responses. So this is simply my share of it. Attachment is formed in many ways, but this concept I present here is crucial to understand. Attachment is formed by grabbing onto, or clutching to, the source of present-moment satisfaction and trying to project it or perpetuate it into an uncertain future. Let's break that down. That source of present-moment satisfaction can be anything, such as a new sexual relationship, a new friend group, a new car, or a new house. It can be anything that brings us a sense of fullness, contentment, or satisfaction. Next, we must understand that we want to keep this newfound joy or happiness in full swing, so what do we do? We try to grab onto our new source of joy and try to control it so that it stays in our lives.

Rather than doing the inner work of becoming our own satisfaction, we love and choose to always take the easy and quick ways to fulfillment. This is the way of the external. This is an extremely negative system of satisfaction because of the reason that the external world is eternally subject to change. So what that means is that if we are clutching tightly to an external person, place, or thing, that brings us joy now, and then that external thing leaves us or changes in some way; now our source of satisfaction that we have become dependent on is gone. This brings us to the next point. We have to understand that people, places, and things are not permanent. They won't be in our lives forever. So we must learn how to go within ourselves, touch the divine spark, and awaken our own internal satisfaction. Concurrently however, we must allow ourselves to fully enjoy and experience what our lives have to offer us in the present moment. If we are constantly worried about keeping someone in our lives, that causes us to constantly work to keep them around. If we are constantly working to keep them around, then that work takes away time from being able to enjoy the present time that we have with them regardless of how long that time is. This is why our time with our pleasures seem "short"; our mind is fractured and divided planning on how to change things around to keep these things in our lives. This applies to all external attachments, not just those with people. Change is a natural part of life. It may hurt at times, but we cannot stop the change. Connecting to our inner divinity and power will lessen the pain of external change.

One of the main reasons people experience things such as depression or perceived anxiety is simply that no inner space has been cultivated. When the external world rejects us in some way, such as if you were to apply for a job and the job rejects you, or if you ask someone on a date and they tell you no, it can be very damaging to our sense of self. Most people do not have that inner connection to self, so, when they are rejected by the world, they are seemingly left with nothing. This causes depression and other negative emotions. When we have cultivated our connection to ourselves to such a depth, the hurt of the outside world is not as hard to go through anymore. We now understand that we always have the strength of ourselves and our eternal divine connection to fall back on. As with many lines in these pages, this again points to the importance of daily spiritual practice, the cultivation of inner awareness and strength.

For now, this is what I leave you with: It all comes down to being willing to make the choice of choosing ourselves, to make the choice of inner awareness and growth over external pain and subjugation. When will we make the change? When will we each make the individual change so the collective may flourish through divine inspiration? These are questions that are left with you.

IX

Foundations of Flow

When farming land, certain factors must be taken into account. Is the land fertile? Are there proper minerals in this area of earth? Will there be enough rain here? How hot does it get, and what type of crops can survive in certain temperatures? There are myriad questions to be asked. The same applies to us when we begin to seek a deeper connection to life, and if we seek to form a deeper connection to the divinity that surrounds us each moment of our lives. If we tried to quickly jump into a deeper, more esoteric path, then because it isn't something we are used to, and because we haven't cultivated space to support such a change, it will be short-lived. This is why many people who choose to make a new year's resolution slowly sink back into old ways of being after some time. It is because the space for growth has not yet been made. It is all a part of our egoic system that makes us want to jump right into something new full-throttle before we have cultivated the necessary foundations.

To begin, we will ask a question: what is meant by the foundations of flow? How can something that flows have a foundation? Simply, this foundation is fundamentally formless; it is an understanding and an action. We must let go of the version of ourselves that is no longer in divine alignment with who we now are. We must understand that the growth we seek can only take root if that which was already there has been excavated in a way. We cannot fill a cup that is already full of a different way of being. We must mourn the past version of ourselves that will soon be all but a memory. When someone close to you passes on, it is quite likely that you will be hurt, and that you will shed tears because that person is gone physically.

This is exactly the same as what is meant here. You must cry and release your old self and your old ways of being. Hold and nurture yourself as you move the watering tears of your past self up and out of your system, so that they may water the seeds of this new awakening version of yourself. Simply, the tears of the old water the seeds of the new. To make this concept of mourning the old or past self easier to grasp, allow this for an example. If you are someone who loves fast food, and your goal is to give up fast food permanently, you must let go of the part of you that loves fast food. You must release the part of you that loves instant gratification and quick stimulation. You must give these parts of yourself up, to make room for the truth. The truth that the universe is not a system of quick stimulation; the truth that the universe is slow, subtle, and medicinal in nature. We must release our love of accepted poison so that we may begin deep healing at a quantum level. You are letting go of that part of yourself, so just as you cry, hurt, and feel uncomfortable when you lose a friend or family member, so too must you cry at the loss and transformation of yourself. These are the bittersweet tears of growth. The part of us that has the urge to eat fast food or be in any other way of existing that we wish to release—we are releasing that part of ourselves, we are taking back control over our habits.

We are becoming aware that our primal urges and desires are not in control. We are becoming aware that our primal urges and desires are simply impulses of the lower mind, or lower self. For the point of clarity within this message, I do mean quite literally, allow yourself to cry. Allow yourself to be in that vulnerable state. The more vulnerable you can be with yourself, the deeper the seed of your growth will be. Unconditionally love those parts of yourself that may have never been loved in that way your entire life. As you are mourning and releasing past ways of being, with each tear that is shed, imagine that old attachment leaving you as well. You will feel as if you have been reborn. Now we have begun to scratch the surface of creating the foundations of flow.

Again, of course, this is easier said than done. The process of mourning, crying, and being emotionally expressive is more difficult for some than it will be for others. It will be especially difficult if you grew up in an environment where your emotions were never acknowledged or properly cared for. There is no time limit for this to take place, and there is no "right" way. As long as you continuously put effort into your self and show up for yourself each day, you will get exactly where you are supposed to be. Do not let the speed of someone else's results affect your emotional state or the choices you make for your own path. Others may be a positive influence for sure, but be aware if someone else's results or success makes you jealous or resentful or makes you question yourself in some way. Everyone is living a life different from the one you are living, with different lessons to be learned. Just that we do not see others struggle does not mean that they are perfect. You are actually incomparable to the person you keep comparing yourself to. You have your own skills just as they have theirs. The story in your own mind that this person is somehow better than you is just another level of your emotional body that needs love given to it. Everyone has or has had some sort of insecurity caused by some type of physical, mental, or emotional trauma that may be stemming all the way from early childhood, or even up to the recent past. Trauma does not only happen when we are young, it has the potential to happen at any age, at any time. This is the very point of this great work. This journey we are on is to heal these parts of ourselves so that we may experience the fullness and bliss that life truly has to offer, beyond our distorted and traumatized filters. We simply must awaken our eye that has been here this entire time. It is easy to understand why we as humans want to jump right into starting something new without creating the proper foundations. First and foremost, we are beings that have been conditioned to not take the slow or methodic way. We constantly consume, we are always looking for the "new thing" to buy, or the new trend to jump on. We don't take things slow because we have been programmed to seek speed, instant gratification, and an overload of stimulation.

This is why we constantly seek more and more. Things that come with great speed never last. So we keep trying to fill that void within. The only way to truly fill that void permanently is to realize that you are the void. That you are energy. That you are an eternal flow of creation. Secondly, as humans, we enjoy speed because speed is a distraction. When you are constantly chasing, doing, and consuming, you are distracted from your own mind and emotions. When we slow down for a moment, our thoughts and emotions become more pronounced and perceivable. That makes us uncomfortable. We don't want to acknowledge our thoughts. So we eat, we have sex, we watch TV, we spend hours in the gym, we drink copious amounts of alcohol, then we sleep, wake up, and do it all over again, as if this were our natural state. We've all at some point joked about the rat race, or the repetitive nature of how we do things every day, but few stop and look deeper into these unnatural cycles we commit ourselves to. It is now exceedingly understandable that we love to go fast in life, but we must learn to slow way, way down. The flow of the universe is of an extremely slow and subtle nature. The higher or deeper dimensions of reality are of a slow and subtle nature. This is why most cannot perceive multi-dimensional reality. It is most certainly not because they are not special. Everyone has these capabilities of perception; some just understand that truth, and consciously work toward it every day. Others choose the easy way of short-lived satisfaction. We must allow the turning of the wheel of the mind to come to a complete stop. Only when we are still will the subtleties of divine reality become knowable to the seeker. In essence, if it is a mystical experience you seek, simply become still of mind, still of body, and surrender all desire and thought; then the mystical or actually the truly ordinary nature of divine life; will become known. For the mystical constantly surrounds each and every one of us at all times; we just need to learn the necessary steps to adjust our perception, and to unblock the eye that is able to see what is already here. We must be willing to slow down and create that space within us that will give us the necessary room to flourish. Seeds must be planted deep in the soil; they do not sit on top of the ground. We must mourn the metaphorical death of how we used to live life in order to create that space for something new to take hold. We cannot expect to gain something without first giving something up. You cannot grow a flower in the exact spot where a weed is growing. You must remove one in order for the other to exist with maximum potential. The situation we find ourselves in within this modern society is that we are, each of us, full of weeds. We have come to love our weeds, however.

We believe we do not need to change, or we believe that we are perfectly fine. However, we subconsciously know that we are full of weeds, and we never look within because we don't want to look at our ugliness. Until we face our ugliness, our uncomfortable past ways of being, our weeds, are here to stay. To understand this metaphor of weeds that represent our internal ugliness or shadow, we will take this a few steps deeper. We must start back with the understanding that in this modern society, everyone is full of this internal shadow, or internal weeds. The predicament comes from the fact that the weeds are now accepted as normal just because everyone has them. We have normalized and accepted this spiritual sickness and lack of awareness as normal, just because everyone is sick. No matter how terrible we feel, we tell ourselves it's okay and that nothing needs to change because "it's how everyone is." To further this delusion, no one has any idea how to excavate the weeds of spiritual sickness and detachment even if they wanted to, simply because of the fact that the tools that are needed are energetic tools, tools of deeper awareness. No one knows how to access their spiritual toolkit anymore. So, to put it together, here we are believing everything is fine because everyone feels and acts the same, and no one has any possible clue on how to cleanse and release the weeds of internal sickness. So it is a double-whammy, layered delusion. "Everything is fine because everyone feels the way I feel, and no one around me is trying to change, or knows how to change, so this must be the correct way of existing." This is why discernment is needed. We must not fear being the first to make the change.

I am quite positive that we have all heard the phrase, "If your friends were jumping off a cliff, would you follow?" So now I ask you, if everyone were heading down a clearly detrimental path, would you be brave enough to stand and say enough? Would you be brave enough to walk alone if that's what it takes? Only you have the answers for yourself.

X

The Hero's Journey

Throughout these pages, we have touched on a myriad of topics, most of which, if not all, drive or point in the direction of self-awareness, spiritual awareness, and personal growth. All of these points describe something we know as the hero's journey. Now, before the word "hero" goes to your head, understand that this is merely a concept. In all great stories, there is a hero and a villain of sorts. The story may start with a prologue about a peaceful time of existence when there was fairness, unconditional love, and equality. Then the villain comes in, an entity bent on some sort of dominance or control over a certain area or realm. Then the peaceful place starts to fall into decay and destruction in response to this seemingly all-powerful villain. Now we meet the hero who will rise to the occasion of standing against the villain, someone who stands for the people. This is where the hero's journey begins. The hero believes themselves strong enough to defeat or apprehend the villain, so they face them, and almost always lose at first. The hero gets destroyed to the extent of near death and destruction, barely escaping with their life. The hero has no choice but to retreat and take into account their failure and how terribly wrong everything went regardless of how they planned.

The hero must then accept that they were wrong, and then they must spend time learning, training, and reinventing themself in order to defeat this mighty villain. This is often done with long periods of solitude or with a mentor of sorts; often, both of these are needed. The relentless challenging of the self, and the challenging of past belief systems, is needed so that the hero may evolve to the point where defeating the villain is not only possible, but likely. The villain in their hubris does not embark on that journey of the soul already having defeated the hero. They do not believe they need to do the inner inquiry and revitalization because they have seen that they have already won and see no need to change. This is why the hero always triumphs when they next face the villain.

So you see, we each are the hero of our own story; we believe we are already smart enough or strong enough, until we are faced with a great adversary. This adversary does not have to be a person. The adversary of our story can be any great challenge in our lives. We can also face collective adversaries such as our collective shadow (we will discuss collective shadow later) our collective unconsciousness, our societal destruction and perceived separation—the list is infinite. We must come to terms with the fact that we will not overcome our greatest struggles without first overcoming ourselves and the old ways we were attempting life. If something defeats us, and we attempt that same path or idea again without first stepping back, reevaluating the situation, and making the necessary changes, we will only find ourselves losing again and again until we try a different route to yield different results.

This takes a great amount of courage to do. To give up everything you thought you knew in order to become a fuller and stronger version of yourself is something most would never even fathom doing. They have subconsciously accepted pain and struggle as the normal way of life, so they do not see a need or reason to bring about change.

This path is supposed to be difficult. If the lessons of life were simple and obvious, it would not be taken seriously, and it would carry less weight. It is the long path that reaps the longer rewards and benefits. It is the path less traveled that has the greatest treasures hidden within. When one studies ancient poetry, more specifically ancient poetry of Eastern influence, one sees that the ancient poet realized that the greatest treasures of life are already within us. We just have not cultivated the eyes to see such a treasure. In much of Rumi's poetry, he tells tales of someone on a great journey to find some great external treasure. Throughout the great journey, the seeker of this treasure is often unsuccessful in their original plans. The seeker then returns home feeling defeated, starts kicking around rocks in their own backyard, and finds gold in their own land! The moral here is that we already possess the great treasure of life, but we are so focused on looking elsewhere that we are blind to our own divine riches. We have allowed ourselves to be influenced by the physical success of others, not asking what it took them to get there, what sacrifices they made, the effort and time they put in. We just want what others have, because we have not yet cultivated a divine relationship to ourselves, so we look outside to fill our void. Again, we have allowed ourselves to be and remain blind and oblivious to the wealth and potential that we each already have. We just do not want to put in the work, effort, and time that others are putting into their success. If one day you sat down and were able to see the full potential of yourself beyond this physical form, you would fall to the ground in awe of yourself. Rumi said something like this: "If I had known the real way it was, I would have stopped all the looking around. But that knowing comes from the time spent looking!" Again, Rumi points to the truth that humans are so lost in this external scramble for wealth and success that the greatest treasure of life is silently collecting dust in the far reaches of their immortal souls. It's as if we've been stuck in a looped video game for so long that we do not care about leaving the game in search of truth any longer, even if the game is poisonous and destructive. This is actually a concept that has been pondered for a great many years. This is the concept of Plato's cave. People have become so hopelessly inured with external life and its stimulation, that the journey of exploring deeper truth isn't even interesting to those who are asleep. This is where we now are as a society. We no longer care for deeper truth as long as we get our cheap comforts that come with a lack of accountability for our world. We just want to sit back in our own patterns and have things given to us. It only starts with us choosing to overcome this sedation and venture into the might of our divine essence, the divine majesty and power of our infinite souls.

The hero's journey requires the courage of leaving your past self, allowing yourself to start over from zero. Most humans, unfortunately, cannot process the importance of this, of being able to allow yourself to start over in order to rebuild withering foundations. We as humans have developed a deep resistance to any sort of change in our lives, but as the seasons change, we must change; the universe is a natural system of ebb and flow, life and death, birth and rebirth. We cannot entirely blame ourselves for this, however; many of our systems today do not teach growth and evolution of the soul. Most, if not all, western religion teaches nothing of meditation, self inquiry, and spiritual awareness. They teach us to put our belief in an external power that will come and save us. As I've said earlier in these pages, this causes us to not take accountability in our own lives for our health, success, and many myriad of other things. The belief that you can just sit back and have someone come take you to heaven defeats the purpose of heaven. There has been no evolution of the soul, evolution that is needed to access the density of heaven. To access or feel the state of "heaven" or "enlightenment," one must become transcendent of all dualities. Otherwise heaven will suffer the same fate as our modern human society. If we did not evolve at the soul level before entering the blissful afterlife, we would still exist with the same spiritual corruption that we have now. For example, we currently as humans love to choose sides and believe we are right. We don't do research, and we blindly follow anything as long as it supports our bias. So if we do not evolve past the need for petty political squabbles, we will still bring that same energy with us after death.

This is why deep evolution of the soul is necessary. It is something that is very possible for each individual to accomplish in life. This also gives an understanding of the concept of samsara, or reincarnation, the cycle of suffering. The hero's journey is taken on by those who have awakened to the fact that there is something more for them to experience, a deeper way of true peace and fulfillment that lasts an eternity. A moment ago I mentioned reincarnation. Allow me to go a little further as to how this is relevant. Now, on the matters of reincarnation there is an infinity that can be said—many, many books' worth. Here, it will be kept brief. Reincarnation plays a crucial role in the evolution of the soul. When a younger soul has incarnated into physical life but has not reached minimal awakening or connection to the self at the spiritual level, then the lessons of life and duality must be experienced again in hopes of completion the next time around. Reincarnation is not needed when a soul has transcended the dualities of illusory physical life.

Reincarnation must not be viewed as something negative. Consider it only as the re-taking of a test that was failed, or a level of a game that must be re-attempted because of incomplete sections. This is how we achieve the level of soul evolution required to advance to the next level of "heaven." It is simply up to us to embark on the hero's journey of growth, evolution, and change. We will face adversaries, we will lose touch with people we believed to be friends or family, but this is part of growth. Remember that everything lost only makes room for what is truly meant to be there. People will judge you for being different, but that is part of the challenge: staying true to yourself regardless of outside opinion. Your true tribe will find you and love you unconditionally. However, you will only meet your true tribe or your soul family when you are truly ready to let go of all limiting beliefs about yourself, your life, and all of your preconceived notions about the possibilities of the future. Your soul family will continue to inspire you to become a better version of yourself. This is why you will only meet them when you are truly ready to do the work. If you, for example, met someone who pushed you to be better, and you were not in the mood to change, you would begin to resent and become annoyed by this person, even though they are clearly on your side. You simply wouldn't be able to see that they are on your side because you are unfortunately still addicted to your old patterns, so this person seems like the enemy trying to pull you into the light, so to speak. When the path of the few is truly embarked on, we must understand that we are awakening the flames of a fire that has all but burnt out. This fire is the connection to ourselves and to the truth of our existence.

As with most things in life, no one can truly awaken, nor commit to this journey, until they themselves are ready for true change. No one can be awakened by someone else; many will remain in a state of deep unconsciousness or self-illusion until their spirit matures to a great enough extent to inspire deeper contemplation that in turn begins the process of self-actualization. Many will inevitably try to explain the experience of awakening to others in order to make them change, but sadly this endeavor almost always comes to naught. As I stated previously, no one can be told of awakening and truly grasp the concepts until their spirit has matured enough to accept radical truth (Or, shall I say, perceived radical truth). We must learn to let go of the desire to forcibly change others, we must enrich our own lives, and we ourselves will become the light of inspiration and change for those around us. The most devastating fires known to man all came from a single spark; it is up to you to become the spark that spreads the engulfing flames of awakening.

XI
Spiritual Bypassing

Many of us, at some point in our lives, whether it be childhood, adulthood, or both, have enjoyed wearing costumes and masks for a certain event, or even just because. It's fun to dress up, hide our faces for a bit, and truly let go, to spend a little time as someone or something else, not worried about being seen, allowing our inner expression to come out more than usual under the guise of a mask. I now ask you this: what happens when that costume becomes a modality of avoidance? What happens when we begin to only focus on the external costume, and not what is happening internally or underneath? Now we begin the discussion of spiritual bypassing.

To begin simply, someone who is spiritually bypassing can be described as someone who cares more about how the outside world perceives them than doing actual inner work. Their spirituality comes in a package, you might say. Often, people who are bypassing true inner work can be found getting a slew of spiritual, chakra-related, or some sort of sacred geometry tattoos. Of course, this does not always represent someone who is bypassing. Tattoos might just be there because they are pretty, and their meaning is revered by their wearer. This is just one thing on the list. Someone who is bypassing may also be found buying many native tools before deeply understanding them. Or they may be found buying a lot of crystals or sage to cleanse negative energy, rather than looking within to release their own negativity. They might even be found buying a lot of trendy clothes to "look more spiritual." Of course, these alone at face value are not for-sure tells that someone is spiritually bypassing. These are just some examples to take in to account that are commonly found. Discernment is our best way to tell if someone is bypassing. People who act high and mighty but are easily triggered are almost always bypassing because of the fact they get easily triggered, which shows a level of internal healing that has yet to take place. Someone's getting offended when someone else tries to correct them is another obvious sign of spiritual bypassing. Now I am not saying it is somehow "bad" to buy things. Not at all. It is great to support native communities and small businesses.

However, we must be very careful not to let these beautiful or shiny external things consume us.

You will plainly be able to tell the difference between a teacher who is neck-deep in true shadow work and a teacher who is spiritually bypassing the inner work. This is why the story of the costume was brought up. People who are bypassing have allowed the costume to become their identity. They've lost themselves. They have become consumed with ego. They love to decorate themselves with labels and paid for achievements. What I mean by "paid for achievements" is, accolades that didn't take much work to achieve, such as paying to take a class and getting an essentially guaranteed certification. This didn't require true inner work, just the possible passing of a general test of some sort. The ego loves these shortcuts, because it allows the self to believe they are doing great work by all of these achievements acquired in a short period of time. This is a sort of spiritualized ego that has merged validation with spiritual awareness. This sometimes makes it tricky because on the outside, at first, they may seem amazing and spiritually attractive, but after conversing with them, you realize the truth at the core of their being. They may say how many healing sessions they've undergone, how many sacred scriptures they've read, or that they are enlightened and others must listen to what they have to say because of the various ascended masters they are "in communication" with. The ego loves to give itself labels and badges to wear, so if someone is very focused on their title, and puts much energy into labels, it's another sign of spiritual bypassing. Healing sessions, psychedelic ceremonies, and that sort of thing are not bad at all to attend. They can hold great benefit for those who attend. We must only be careful to take the time after each healing session or ceremony to integrate what we have experienced, to understand the lessons that were given to us.

Those bypassing who attend such ceremonies think that they just need to attend more ceremonies to be healed, but that is far from the truth. Spending time in meditation to understand what they were shown is the key of all of these modalities. People who are bypassing prefer external satisfaction and shallow validation. A true seeker or someone doing the shadow and soul work will take extended breaks and sit in times of quiet and solitude to allow for deep integration to occur. That is because the true seeker knows and understands that true healing comes from sitting with themselves in times of silence to learn about their shadows and patterns. Sitting in silence and contemplation also allows them to tap into what steps of change they can make in their lives to become a fuller embodiment of their divine nature and essence.

To the rest of the world, the true seeker will seem to be someone who has taken great strides to make positive change in their life, someone who has a noticeable change in habits, patterns, and how they generally show up in the world. Often times also, the true seeker is quiet about their life and what plans they have for the future most of the time. They do not have the need to shout their goals to anyone who will listen. They are quite content with less or no external validation or opinion. The one who is bypassing will be quite opposite most of the time. They may be quite vocal about their goals and achievements as they enjoy external validation, and the worship they may get from others. Those who go the route of bypassing often will tell others that they are some sort of "chosen one." They may try to correct someone else's life when their opinion was never asked for. They believe the more they do on the outside, the more healed they will become. This is dangerous because all of the external things they do in search of healing makes them believe they are healing because of how much effort they are putting into whatever it is that they are doing.

This also prevents them from looking inward because they now believe themselves to be healed. Again though, we must understand that true healing comes from the slow internal work, so that the patterns of the soul may become visible so that we can consciously perceive where we must personally make and commit to a certain change in an area of our lives. It is not my intention here to speak negatively about those who are in a state of spiritual bypassing. Actually, many who embark on a journey of true awareness end up being a perpetuator of spiritual bypassing at one point or another. It is often an unconscious act. My point here is only to bring awareness to this subject, and so that we can honestly learn to check in with ourselves to see whether we are doing the true work or are staying with surface-level commodities. This chapter is to increase our discernment of our selves and when building relationships with others who are seemingly "like-minded." It is crucial that we maintain a high level of discernment when cultivating relationships, especially in the beginning phases of an awakening journey. We want more than anything to find people to talk to about what we are experiencing and going through. This desire makes us overlook certain things sometimes. Just the fact that someone seems to have similar interests to yours at first glance doesn't mean they would be good for you. Discernment and honesty with yourself is key. Discernment will also be key here because there are individuals who seek to use others for their own agendas, full of coercion and manipulation. The seeking of validation and the illusions of ego have even found their way into the most sacred of places. So how do we tell if someone is authentic? We have gone over a few key differences earlier on in this chapter, but briefly we will touch on it once more. Simply look at the life and habits of people. The true seeker will have a slower, simpler, more in tune, and gentle way of being. Someone bypassing will often make themselves seem larger than life, and they often use big fancy words to further their costumed spirituality. These can be such things as constantly talking about energy, alignment, high vibration, frequency, chakras, imbalance—the list goes on. These are by no means somehow bad to talk about; in fact these are intriguing to learn about and discuss, but when these things become our identity is when we need to be careful. The words eventually lose their power and become an empty shell of what they once were. This is how new-age culture hijacks spirituality, by saying whatever is trendy to seem like they are "cool." They are dependent on the external way they are perceived, so they make themselves seem, in a way, "hyper-spiritual." The universe is a system of slow and subtle motion, so this externally aggressive way of being is almost always a clear sign of bypassing. Some more signs of bypassing are the perpetuation of and refusal to release negative habits related to inner healing, shadow work, health, diet, and overall well-being. A person who is more conscious can usually be found having more positive habits relative to the aforementioned items. In the end, it is ultimately left up to us to decide who we work with, build with, and follow. There are many different people on many different paths. Learning discernment will help you build relationships that are mutually beneficial and long-lasting. By this point, you will have known your worth, you will have established your mental and emotional boundaries. Anyone who oversteps or doesn't align with your values can be faced in whatever way you decide is beneficial to the protection of yourself, what you love, and everything in your life.

XII

Duality

We have touched briefly throughout these pages on the concept of duality, but now we will go as deep as is necessary to impress and understand this most fundamental concept of this physical experience. As we dive into the concept of duality, I encourage you to take heed, as the majority of problems we face in modern society stem from the lack of awareness of the illusion that duality creates in our minds. So to start, how can duality be described? This is one of those things about which I like to say, "If you asked ten different philosophers you would get ten different answers." So again, this is my part on the matter. Duality is the enhanced polarization between two opposing forces that are of near equal power, but seemingly separate. Early in beginningless time, before all of creation, there was nothing. There was the void, pure emptiness, nothingness. Then, nothing became aware of itself. Thus, consciousness begins again. As eternal space becomes aware of itself, and begins to explore itself, moving about in thoughtless form, light is awakened. Now duality becomes prominent. The antithesis of dark is light. Through this new light that has awakened, the contrast has been born, and awareness of the dark is now possible. Duality between dark and light is now established. Further examples of duality can be seen as follows: consciousness and unconsciousness, love and hate, purity and corruption, bravery and cowardice. Duality is all around us; there are infinite examples of duality, as there are infinite perspectives of existence.

An unconscious or un-awakened mind is a very dangerous thing where duality is concerned. Someone who is not able to consciously transcend the illusions of duality will then unconsciously continue to perpetuate separation among humanity while believing they are doing the "right" thing. One of the greatest examples of duality is the nature of "right" and "wrong." The matter of right vs. wrong can be entirely chalked up to a system of perspective. One group or person believes they know best, and the other group or person thinks that they know best. Now we find ourselves stuck in the eternal loop of separation. We see this greatly demonstrated in the political squabble between right-wing conservatives and left-wing liberals. Each side believes that they know what is best for the country based on whatever system of belief or mental upbringing they've had in life. Changing the minds of these individuals is a near impossible task because they exist in an unconscious state of awareness. So they remain unaware of the illusory patterns of duality and continue to cause and perpetuate more fighting and arguing. Both sides here are focused on the success of one side, or one "wing," if you will.

Those who transcend duality will understand that to advance as a unified society, we need to learn how to focus on the entire bird, not just our individual wing that we agree with. Each side is as correct and incorrect as their opponent is. That is why this squabble is perpetual, because they are one and the same, but they fight as if separate. Even though peanut butter is very different from jelly, both are needed to create the famous sandwich. Every coin has two sides; both sides are needed, and can't exist without the other. Duality begins to become transcended through practices of introspection and contemplation.

Higher wisdom of the universe is constantly flowing through each and every one of us. When we quiet our minds, we will hear this silent language of instruction, and we will become a collective that is led by the influence of the universe, or divine will, instead of humans making decisions from a place of bias, ego, self-interest, and individual mental conditioning. Regardless of what religion you practice or what political party you identify with, there is something that exists beyond all of these minimal labels and groups. It is the divine blueprint of creation. It is inherent within every cell, every molecule, every atom of this existence. When we have an ego-transcending practice, or duality-transcending practice such as meditation or yoga, we begin to be able to perceive beyond the illusion of our human perception. We begin to awaken the perception of the soul. As the well-known philosopher Alan Watts put it, "the saved need the damned." The saved need the damned order to know where they stand. What he means here is that if we do not have our opposite, we cannot know who or what we truly are, because there is no resistance or contrast. The religious people need people who aren't religious in order for them to know they are in fact religious. Otherwise, it would be an all-encompassing constant and we would have no concept of religious vs. non-religious because everyone would be practicing religion. So there would be no possible way to know the depth of religiousness without there being non-religiousness. So we actually need the person or group we view as our enemy or our opposite, just as they need us, even if we don't want to accept it. The hero will not know he is a hero without the intensity of a villain. Without juxtaposition or contrast, there is little to no awareness of the depth of ourselves and our inner systems. In this same way, we would not know light without darkness. We need the contrast of darkness in order to know the truth of light. The same is true that we need the contrast of light to fully know the darkness. Without darkness, light would simply be an unknown constant. So in a way, duality and all of its illusions heightens and intensifies our physical experience by allowing us to look more deeply into the nature and workings of existence. A final vivid example of this again, in our modern society: those who are Democrat need those who are Republican to exist; otherwise they would not be able to fully know the extent of their beliefs, and how far they are willing to go, and what lines will they cross or won't cross. The Republicans need the Democrats for the same reasons. If only one party existed, they would be existing unchecked, they would inevitably become tyrants, and then they would have become the very thing they intended to destroy. So sure, this may sound great to some, being the only party, but this would cause infinitely more damage than prosperity, because there would be no challenger to check the processes and hold those accountable. Here we will begin to peer into the truth that is higher wisdom; all of these parties are of human creation, inherently illusory and dualistic in nature.

This is why it is imperative that we learn about the illusions of duality, to understand why this game of sides is holding us back from our divine evolution, and our place as a unified galactic civilization. The base truth here is that there are no sides; our traumas, upbringings, and societal conditionings have made us choose a side because we never looked beyond the surface level of reality. We just did what we were told for centuries because that is all we knew. We were very off-track with that way of mind. Anyone who votes in or partakes in or gives their time and energy in any way to promote this system is unaware of the dualistic illusory nature of reality, so they restrict themselves unconsciously to their one side, thus putting a halt on the unification of the collective.

Advanced civilizations of old achieved their status because they understood there are no such things as sides. There is only higher philosophy based on the three concepts of unconditional love, sovereignty, and compassion. Ancient groups such as the Egyptians, Sumerians, and those in the Americas achieved their architectural and technological feats through the pooling and sharing of knowledge and resources, not separating, hoarding and hiding things from other groups. This is our current problem in modern society. We love keeping secrets and hiding what we know from our "enemy" so that "our side" can "win." Until we can trash this way of being, we will stay with the sickness we now face. Current humans love to fight against those who are not in their "party," and then they go around and speak that they love and accept all. Unfortunately this is just lip service to make themselves feel better about their chosen life path. You cannot speak vulgar hatred of other humans and then claim that you are loving and peaceful. I risk sounding redundant with this point, but it is crucial to grasp. Each side must awaken to the fact that they have been duped. They must awaken to the fact that they are only one side of the coin, but they have believed themselves to be the entire coin, or the only "right" way. Finding Substantial answers for modern problems in ways of being such as these past systems is logically impossible. A coin will always have two sides, but there will only ever be one coin. Both sides are equally needed to form one creation. The systems of limitation must be transcended and let go of. No excuses, no fear, just ultimate surrender to divine will. We must return to the connection we had with nature in the days of old.

We have secluded ourselves into boxes, we cut down our environments, we kill the wildlife, and we think ourselves the masters of the earth. A great humbling shall soon fall upon us if we do not learn to humble ourselves first. Perennial philosophy flows through all of nature, so of course we have lost our way if we have cut ourselves off from the very thing that was meant to teach, guide, and nurture our existence. There is unlimited natural energy to be learned and harnessed.

This is the energy that fundamentally shaped all ancient civilizations that are technologically advanced in a way that we scarcely understand. This is the higher system that transcends all dualities of this illusory world. This is the system we must realize within ourselves through meditation. Just the fact that we humans have forgotten this ancient wisdom does not mean that it is not still there, pulsing through all of creation. Just because you forget you have a bike doesn't mean the bike disappears. It might take some time to get used to again, but it never left you. It will take time to usher in this deeper way of being, but it will inevitably feel natural and beautiful because it is the truth at our core. It is when the beings that were trusted with stewardship of the earth become its destroyers that we have collectively failed. Yes. We have collectively failed. No one will do the work for you or for me. No religious person or figure is coming to save us, no politician or political party will fix everything; it is us. You and I are the saviors we have been waiting for. The illusion of duality is a metaphorical door that has been closed but left unlocked. All we must do is choose to open it and walk through. Most modern humans believe that they do not have the capacity to achieve such states of purity and wisdom. This is far from the truth. We already exist in those higher realms; we have just unconsciously clouded our own vision. We must embark on the great journey of clearing our higher perception. We will then see the truth that has been with us this entire time. All life has the potential for self-actualization and awakening. Pay attention here, as I said this is called "self-actualization," meaning it must be done by you, the self. No one can come do it for you. When we sit back waiting for the job to be "taken care of," we are deluding ourselves and slowing our own evolution. Whether we choose to devote the time to our self-actualization is another story. Just the fact that someone chooses to prioritize comfort and stimulation over inner work and awakening does not mean they do not have the capacity; it means that they are still unconsciously locked in a system of avoidance and ignorance of truth. Many will try to say they aren't capable simply because the thought of changing their life is daunting to them. So again, we are presented with an example of how modern structures have caused many of us to be comfortable sitting back while everything burns, and act like nothing is happening. Again, the decision to step beyond illusion lies with each of us individually. What are we willing to sacrifice to find truth?

XIII

Awakening the Etheric Heartbeat

We are all aware to some extent, (at least I hope we are) of our physical heart and heartbeat. We are aware of its purpose to send oxygenated blood throughout our bodies so that we may continue functioning as we are designed to. What if I were to say that the physical heart and heartbeat are not the only centers of energy that exist, and that they are not the only centers that need our devoted attention? The heartbeat of our energetic body is just as important as, if not more important than, our physical heart.

The ether, the akasha, the causal realm—all of these names are synonyms for one perennial meaning: the realm of spirit, the dimensions of nature that exist beyond our limited human perception of reality. These are the realms of extra-sensory perception. We, each of us, are constantly existing in these multi-dimensional realms of reality through our soul, spirit, and energy, even if we cannot always perceive them. Our extra-sensory perception is governed primarily through the pineal gland, otherwise known as the "third eye." This is an actual organ that is no bigger than a few grains of rice, and it is located in the brain, between the *colliculi superiores* of the *lamina tecti*, at the back of the posterior wall of the third ventricle. Just the fact that we cannot perceive these domains of existence through the normal happenings of our standard perception does not make them any less real.

It can be unhealthy or dangerous to an extent to not be aware of yourself to these depths; allow me to explain. As we covered earlier, our soul, our spirit, and our consciousness exist eternally in these deeper realms or dimensions. To not have a conscious connection to, awareness of, and relationship to these levels of ourselves opens us up to the possibility of spiritual or psychic attack and manipulation or coercion by other entities that have this awareness. This is analogous to leaving your bank account unsecured or open, or leaving your safe unlocked, or your car door open. When we are not aware that an aspect of ourselves exists, it allows it to be influenced and manipulated by those who have deeper spiritual knowledge.

"Have you ever sensed that our soul is immortal and never dies?"
—Plato

There are higher forces all around us, and they are not all positive. I do not say this to instill fear; I say this to bring attention to the importance of self-awareness in all of its depths and angles. We must learn to slow down and transcend our physical heartbeat so that we may begin to awaken and tap into what I call the etheric heartbeat, the heartbeat of eternal creational power that we all have flowing through us. This will open us up to a much darker line of thought—that being the fact that there are entities and beings that exist that seek the power of our souls for their own agendas. That is why there is much darkness in certain realms of humanity. The manipulation, the corruption, the mind control of the masses through mainstream news and media—the depth of what is currently going on has scarcely entered the average person's darkest nightmares. If we do not consciously align with these dimensions of ourselves, it gives free rein then for darker or negatively oriented beings and forces to feed on our energy.

When these negative forces attach themselves to us, it manifests as our being drained, depressed, unmotivated, and even sick seemingly out of nowhere. When we are in alignment with these aspects of ourselves, strength is built, wisdom is attained, energy is strengthened, and we are not easily manipulated, or taken advantage of, by evolved darker forces. This is, again, meant not to create fear, but rather to stress the importance of true self-understanding to our deepest extents that go beyond this physical level of reality that we have identified ourselves with. There are many dimensions that exist in this reality; simply that our physical form exists in the third dimension or frequency does not mean that we cannot learn and acquire the tools to perceive and work with the higher aspects of ourselves. This applies to all humans regardless of religious beliefs. Quantum physics has well proven the existence of multi-dimensional or multi-layered reality. So just as we care for ourselves physically by eating nutritious foods, exercising, and taking care of our mental health, we must learn and adopt spiritual practices that connect us to and nurture ourselves at the spiritual and soul level. We can procrastinate and tell ourselves that we do not have the capacity of this awareness, but the truth is, we all have this capacity. Most just choose instant gratification and mental and physical stimulation over the slow, treasure-filled, beautiful journey of soul evolution. This is an inevitable transformation of all beings; some will be more willing to surrender their plans, expectations, and ego sooner than others, but inevitably evolution must occur within every being.

As the etheric heartbeat is awakened, extrasensory perception or mystical experience comes much more frequently and grows with vivid power. This is because we are opening our minds, surrendering expectations, and returning to the deep connection to nature. The awakened etheric perception is not the only benefit of awakening. Life itself will seem to become reinvigorated, a renewed, childlike sense of wonder will be a new normal, a thirst for new experiences will arise, and a sense of infinite confidence in yourself will come with connecting to your divine authority. Another benefit is a love of life, a deeper comprehension of what it truly means to be unconditionally loving and compassionate beyond just what we tell ourselves. These are needed understandings if society is to advance. This is why I made the point earlier that the evolution of the soul is inevitable for each and every one of us. Whether it is embarked upon in this lifetime or the next, it must take place. Much of our extrasensory perception has been lessened as of late because of the amount of poison that is found in most food in this modern day. The pineal gland can become calcified from contact with certain chemicals and toxins, inhibiting our innate spiritual awareness. This is partially why many believe themselves to have less of a powerful capacity. In all actuality, it is simply the poison we have come to accept, even love, no matter how damaged our health becomes. This poison has blocked our deeper spiritual perception, and our divine knowledge. We must release our love of poison.

There are many teachings and writings about the decalcification of the pineal gland that can be looked into, so we don't need to go too far into it here. Two methods that are key that I will mention, however, are the use of breath work and the avoidance of fluoride. Breath work is an often-used method of decalcification, and it works because the lungs produce the exact same compound that is produced in the pineal gland, called dimethyltriptamine, or DMT. This compound is also found in a wide variety of flora species. This is a naturally occurring substance that produces powerful visual experiences. When deep breath work is initiated for a decent length of time, it creates a cyclical flow of energy between the lungs and the pineal gland, and throughout the entire body. Throughout this cyclical breathing pattern, this flow that is created can be simply understood in its decalcification power as a river that withers down rock and earth over time. We increase this flow of divine awakened energy, and toxins are in a way "washed off" in this energetic flow of chi or breath.

I also mentioned the avoidance of fluoride as a method of decalcification. This is because this chemical, found in common household toothpaste, is known to powerfully block and inhibit pineal operations. The pineal gland exists outside of the blood-brain barrier, making it unique, but it is also the most fluoride- and calcium-saturated organ of the body. When this organ is saturated by these, it can cause a variety of failures such as melatonin deficiency. Melatonin deficiencies can cause a variety of effects on the body, all the way from perceived anxiety to immune suppression associated with cancer. This chemical in our toothpaste is destroying our internal systems, and yet we use it every day, sometimes multiple times per day, and it is found in our drinking water and in our showers and baths. Unless we are using some sort of filtration system, we are being drenched in these chemicals. We must not allow ourselves to believe it is we who are incapable. It is the amalgamation of the chemicals and toxins in our food, and things we regularly use that are poisoning and destroying our internal systems thus destroying our deep spiritual awareness and connection to ourselves. It is the amount of sugar, fast food, processed food, additives, and preservatives that the average person consumes that is the reason that higher perception is blocked, not that we are incapable. If we wish to break the cycle of war, destruction, poverty, and sickness, then it must be we who break the cycle of negative habits in our own lives at the individual level.

Take this moment to briefly ask yourself these questions, and maybe even write your answers down so you can build a plan to work on them: "What negative or unhealthy habits do I have?" "What are my eating habits like?" "How often do I watch TV or movies?" "Do I consume fast food, processed food, greasy food, or alcohol on a regular basis?" "Do I hang around people who influence me to grow, or hold me in the past?" These are some of the questions we must be brave enough to ask ourselves if we wish to spark change or growth in our lives. With habits, it must be a clean break; "a little bit here or there" are famous last words. That's the same as saying "I'll just have a little bit of poison now; it's fine." That's outlandish to say the least. If we wish for the flowers of evolution to spark within us, we cannot keep holding onto the weeds that are blocking the space of the flower. This takes bravery and commitment to accomplish—bravery to begin the journey of letting go your old self and ways of being and commitment because you must be devoted each day to building the foundation for your new self and to resist the constant temptation of processed foods and the infinite amounts of mental and physical stimulation that surround us today.

As we begin invoking change in our lives, we must remember that the universe operates of a slow and subtle nature. This means we cannot expect results overnight or even in the first week. Decades of unhealthy patterns take time to repair. That is the beauty of this journey. Each day, a new treasure of yourself will be known. As we slow down, and return to natural true ways of being, our divine authority and essence will become known to us. The beauty of our true nature, when connected to, will cause tears of awe, bliss, and divine ecstasy. To experience such states comes with a price. The price is what we have been talking about here. The price is our old habits, our negative and unconscious patterns, and our addiction to stimulation over stillness. The old ways of being must be mourned and released back to the universe; we must grieve at the loss of our old selves and cry the bittersweet tears so that our sacred space may be cleared for the new, to allow universally aligned versions of ourselves to begin taking hold and manifesting into physical reality. For this to be possible, it must be *known* that it is possible. If we continuously think ourselves small, weak, and incapable, then of course nothing will change. The first step is to know that the seemingly impossible is in fact, very possible. We must surround ourselves with those who know that what we think is impossible can actually be achieved. Thus our mindset about what is truly possible changes. The ever-expanding doorway to our own soul becomes more and more accessible and vivid the more we commit to this vision of our true divine nature and capability. There are many people surrounding us, closer than we may think, who are eager and waiting to assist us on this journey, many who have already gone through many stages of this awakening experience and have dedicated years of time as way-showers for a new world. We must only humble ourselves enough to know we don't have the answers; we must only be humble enough to ask.

XIV

Fundamentals of Shadow Work

When the phrase "shadow work" first hits your eyes or ears, what is the immediate thought that you have? Many might think of things in the realm of witchcraft, or the occult. Some might even believe it to have an evil or satanic meaning. In the sense we will be discussing here, none of the aforementioned descriptions are accurate. We will uncover now what is meant by "shadow." The shadow as we mean it here can be described in many ways; it can mean the subconscious and unconscious mind, the wounded inner child, the far depths of our mental and emotional bodies, so on and so forth. So, what is meant in totality by the esoterically common phrase "shadow work" is work that is done in relation to these deep parts of ourselves that we otherwise ignore. Why would someone need to undergo shadow work? Those who choose to consciously align with the infinite mission that is shadow work, do so with the intent of the deeper exploration of the self on all levels. In a way, the shadow can be described as the unconscious self, the parts of us that have been running on autopilot, our conditioned self.

FUNDAMENTALS OF SHADOW WORK

Those on the journey of true shadow work seek to liberate themselves from an unconscious way of being. We have covered the unconscious way of being at different parts throughout this writing, but now we will tie it together with shadow work. The unconscious way of being is simply the robotic way most of us cope through life seemingly on autopilot. One day we ask ourselves where our life went. Shadow work is a key factor in all journeys of those who wish to become a fuller and better version of themselves. That is why this part has been given the name "The Fundamentals of Shadow Work": to help all who truly seek the tools for a fuller sense of self. Now, before we dive in, it is important to understand that every single being alive is in need of shadow work, as I've said before. I am not interested in how spiritually enlightened you claim yourself to be; if you were complete in your self-knowledge, you would fully become dematerialized from the physical world.

If you achieved such a state, there would be no more need for you to be on this planet because you attained full self-knowledge. Humble the ego, and shadow work can begin. We all need shadow work, and if we didn't need it, then our collective would be united as one race. As we can all see, we are not united even on the basic levels, so therefore the deep work is still needed. In fact, the ones who say they don't need shadow work are typically the ones who will benefit the most from this work. Anyone who says they do not need it is simply still a victim of their own ego's refusing to take accountability. We must be willing to look at ourselves in this uncomfortable way. So, with that being said, let us begin.

On the matters of bravery and courage, these are critical in shadow work. You will be confronted with your own mind, your past, your darkest thoughts, and your deepest emotions. You will be shown what toxic or negative habits you continue to perpetuate in your own life, and therefore in the collective. You will be called out, and you will be held accountable in a way that you most likely never have been in your entire life. This is not something fun or cool or comfortable. In true shadow work, your ego will be put in check. Your ego will be screaming bloody murder for you to go back to the ways of avoidance. You will be faced with many hard truths about your own life and our collective reality. Those who possess the bravery and courage to accept truth that goes against or contradicts their previous belief systems or ways of being have now begun to scratch the surface of true shadow work. This is not meant to scare or push anyone away from shadow work; this is meant to prepare and provide fundamental insight and awareness of possibilities that are extremely and immensely common in this work. Here we must also state that the benefits of a massive release of past traumas, coping mechanisms, and unconscious and unhealthy ways of being far outweigh a bit of time spent being uncomfortable.

Life becomes reinvigorated, the lust of true wonder is reawakened, the heavy and illusory filters are now gone, and we have the ability to experience the depth of ourselves and a depth of life that has not been experienced because we were full of unconsciousness and toxicity we never knew was there. Shadow work can be plainly described as deep introspection. Periods of solitude are needed for the exploration of the self. Although it is great and amazing to have and experience friendships, extended periods of quiet and stillness are required as well, to experience our own consciousness and ways of being contrasted against the true flow and blueprint of divine creation. This is a hard truth for some to hear; someone who has never known periods of solitude and who has become addicted to being around others will struggle with extended solitude at first, as this is the antithesis of the ways they are used to living life. Needing to be around others as a source of happiness and joy simply shows a level of emotional healing that is needed within the self. Constantly surrounding ourselves with the energy of others allows us to turn our focus away from ourselves. We do this because we subconsciously do not want to look at our own ugliness. When life gets quiet, our internal happenings become louder and more vivid, and that is uncomfortable to the unconscious person. So we seek a myriad of coping mechanisms to drown out our internal self such as drinking, drugs, sex, partying, food, TV, surrounding ourselves with others—even the gym can be an unhealthy coping mechanism if it's being used to take the mind away from the self and the needed emotional work. We must let go of the outside world for long periods at a time. The reason for this is that in those deep states of solitude and awareness, the subtle song and flow of God, or of the universe, comes into tangible perception. This allows us to take an honest look at our own ways of being, contrasted against the now perceivable higher way of existence, or the laws of divine order. For example, while in solitude and contemplation or meditation, the universe can be found to speak to us in those states of deep stillness. As we observe the subtle language of the universe, we can reflect on our own lives and see how we essentially "stack up" compared with this sort of "divine" or "higher" law that we can now tangibly perceive in meditation. This is how we release old ways of being and align ourselves with our spiritual essence as beings of divine authority. Shadow work will inevitably connect us home to our true divine nature, thus allowing us to unite with one and other regardless of differences or belief systems, because again, we will have attained a higher level of awareness and alignment with an aspect of ourselves that is beyond physical. So our egos and political biases will fall away as leaves do in autumn. This happens because consciousness has begun to awaken to its own nature beyond primitive limitations, so it does not concern itself with such things as limited human egos and biases. So concurrently, because we have aligned in some way with this "higher mind," we too will no longer care about these things. Thus the collective transcends these illusory divisive concepts, and we unify as one.

This is because of the fact that each of us is beyond human. This may be hard to accept for some, but this is why spiritual practice and introspection are of the utmost importance. It connects us to our divine nature. We are spirits, so we each must create our own spirituality—not one that has been sold to us and manipulated for the benefit of the few through the endless hunger of capitalism. It must now be understood that in the same way we each have individual shadows to explore, there is also something known as the collective shadow or collective unconscious. What is the collective shadow? The collective shadow is the unconscious manifestation or reflection of darkness that is created by the cumulative shadows of each person in our world. When all of our unconscious selves or shadows join together on a large scale, you get the collective shadow. We increase and perpetuate a darker, more uncomfortable, more chaotic and destructive collective shadow by not taking accountability in our own lives. Each of us is responsible for a piece of the collective unconscious, and through the journey of deep healing at the individual level, we bring great healing to the collective shadow, and our reality will reap the benefits. Now, don't think you must take a great stand and become an influencer on social media or something. You do not need to do anything of the sort unless you are truly called to do such a thing. All that is needed is an open mind and the willingness to spend great deals of time in your own life humbly exploring yourself and asking the tough questions. You must be willing to accept truths that may be hard to hear at first, truths that you have been refusing to look at your entire life. As we each begin to do this work for ourselves, we release and heal our part of the collective shadow and our new energy inspires our neighbors to do the same, and then eventually the truth that has been hidden from humanity will inevitably come into the light. Fear of the unknown will no longer exist because of the fact that we have faced the unknown by facing ourselves.

To make this even more comprehensible, I will use a simple analogy. Imagine, if you will, a pizza the size of a table that equals about fifty regular slices when cut. It is a daunting task to attempt to complete this process of eating this pizza alone. This pizza represents the collective shadow. It seems impossibly large and unfathomable for one or two people to face alone. Now, when you have fifty people, or an amount of people sufficient for everyone to be responsible for a small share, the task goes from seemingly impossible to easily doable. We each must be willing to accept and face the amount of unconsciousness that we contribute to the collective shadow. We must each eat our slice of the pie. In this modern society, we have grown comfortable and complacent sitting around for a seemingly infinite amount time while everything is burning, waiting for some religious savior or political figure to fix the world for us. What we have not grasped is the fact that the longer we sit back staying in our same patterns, the larger the collective shadow grows, and the more uncomfortable it will be to face later on. Humanity is now primed and at the perfect time to begin this deep introspective work. We have yet to simply sit down for a moment and honestly ask ourselves about our own lives, to ask ourselves why we are the way we are and to allow the possibility of an entirely new system of awareness. A main reason most humans do not embark on a journey of truth such as this is that there is a fear of starting over. It is just too much for them to even entertain the thought that they could have been unconscious their entire lives and they must revamp their entire way of being. It does not need to seem as drastic or as daunting as this. The universe is a system of slow and subtle change. So all that is essentially needed is small commitment that grows over time. Begin with simple small self-inquiries, and honestly answer them to yourself. Then, as time goes on, and truth becomes more comfortable, the devotion and commitment naturally grows and becomes stronger, because the real you is now able to emerge from the shadows of your unconscious self, and you will witness the re-awakening of your inherent nature. The thirst for deeper awareness and divine union becomes who you are, or rather, it simply becomes more visible, because this has always been a truth at our core as inherently divine beings. You become someone who has fallen in love with knowing the true beauty, depth, divinity, and majesty of life. We must not be too concerned with what other people are doing in their respective lives; we must focus on our own growth and becoming the inspiration that encourages others to embark on deeper journeys of awareness. A roaring fire may spread through an entire city but was only begun by a single meager spark. We each have a divine spark within us that possesses the potential to spread the purging fires of awareness.

Shadow work is not something that is meant to be pretty. True shadow work involves pain, crying, internal adversity, and struggle. For those who remain on this journey throughout the hardship, the greatest spiritual, mental, emotional, and physical release awaits you. We face the past, and the depths of ourselves, so that those shattered parts of our psyche and emotional body may be reintegrated, and all that needs to leave our system to make room for the new will be released. There is an old Zen saying from Lao Tzu: "If you wish to be given everything, give everything up." If we wish to have a life full of fulfillment, joy, peace, success, abundance, and bliss, we must first be willing to give up our old habits and mental coping mechanisms. It is only through the surrender of these aforementioned things that the new and stronger version of ourselves will have the necessary space to take hold and flourish. Those who embark on this journey are often outcasts in one way or another. Those who speak truth in a world of lies will often be looked at as insane.

"Those who are able to see beyond the shadows and lies of their culture will never be understood, let alone believed, by the masses." —Plato

The course must be stayed either way. To anyone who has read this far, there is a high chance you have begun this journey and you are looking to further your awareness in some way, or you are curious at least in how to begin this journey and now are seeking the tools and foundations. You feel the call to awaken your true connection to reality. Either way, it is a moment to commend yourself for. You are going against the grain of society in search of the deeper truth. Many could not, and will not, take this step. It is your continued effort and devotion that will inspire others to make change as you have and seek the deeper joy that life has to offer. The following are just some of the infinite questions we may begin to ask ourselves to spark and deepen the shadow work journey. These questions should be asked while in times of stillness and contemplation. With these questions we must keep an open mind, for we may not like the answers that we find. This however, is why it is so important; growth comes when we accept that we are wrong or that a change needs to be made after deep introspection.

- Are my beliefs truly mine? Or are they a product of what my parents forced on me? If these are my parents' or guardians' beliefs, are these beliefs I want to keep, and why do I want to keep them?
- Have I experienced any mental, emotional, or physical trauma that could possibly be distorting my perception and views of reality? If so, what am I doing to release said trauma?
- How do I speak to myself and treat myself? Do I say things such as "I'm not good enough" or "I'm not worthy" or "I'm not pretty" or "I'm so stupid" or "I hate my life"? If I am saying anything similar to these statements, am I working to become more conscious of it, and am I working to reprogram my subconscious through positive speech and affirmation?
- How do I speak to other people or my pets? Am I aware how my words affect them? Do I call people mean names, do I tell jokes I don't mean, do I call my pets bad or tell them they are bad when they are not? If so, what can I do or say instead of things that are mean or negative, even if they are meant as a joke?
- What negative or unconscious patterns do I have in my life? How much time do I spend seeking stimulation or pleasure? How often and how many hours a day do I watch TV or movies or scroll on my phone? How much processed or artificial or fast food do I consume? What am I truly doing to release these patterns from my life permanently?
- Do I consistently put others before myself? Do I feel that their needs are more important than my own? If so, how can I validate and empower myself to be able to say no when I

don't have energy, and to strongly know that my needs deserve to be one of my top priorities, if not at the very top?
- Am I actually working to better myself, or am I just telling myself that I am, while doing minimal work and keeping most of my unhealthy habits? If so, how can I be more true to myself and actually put forth true commitment to growing as a person?
- Is there anyone in my life who makes me feel uncomfortable or insecure when I am around them? If so, why do they make me feel insecure, and how can I learn to become more comfortable in my own skin and be able to fully release this insecurity?
- Are the people I surround myself with focused on becoming better versions of themselves? Or do they hold the same unconscious patterns that I am trying to release—or worse ones? How consciously aware are the people I hang out with? Are these people going to benefit my mental, emotional, and spiritual growth? If they are not of benefit to my life in these ways, how can I begin to release them from my life?
- Am I someone who enjoys the feeling of fitting in and being liked? Do I often bite my tongue or hold my words back because I do not want others to cast me out? Do I enjoy receiving my validation from others before giving myself validation? If so, how can I work on validating myself so that I am self-empowered and comfortable speaking my truth regardless of how others will view me or treat me?

Simply pick one of these questions at a time, meditate on the question, and allow your soul to give you an answer. Again, we must be open to even the answers we do not want to hear. No one is perfect; that is why we are on this journey. There is no judgment here. After receiving your answer, you will be able to make a change, or remain with the same patterns. The choice is yours alone.

XV

Meditation Tools

These are simply some of the basic tools I have learned to be quite helpful in meditation in my years of embarking on this journey.

On the beginnings of meditation:
- *Allow your body to move and shift around.* This allows you to find the position that will allow for the longest meditative state possible. If we are uncomfortable, our mind may continuously be taken out of presence.
- *Check in with the breath, mind, and body.* This allows us to have a deeper awareness of ourselves and any areas that have pain or discomfort and that may need to be addressed in some way. This also allows us to take notice of where our thoughts are and will allow us to slowly release said thoughts and if we need to deepen or soften the breath, and it lets us tune into the deeper needs of the body, as we previously covered.

- *Release all attachments and worries of physical life; forget anything that is physical.* This allows us to deepen our energetic presence, to make room for us to experience our nature beyond the physical, as souls and spirits. There is time to ponder physical life later. Your meditation is for you to go beyond your physical self and connect to your energetic self.
- *Allow the breath to deepen and the mind and body to become still.* When these aspects of ourselves become slow and still, we will have an easier time tapping into the beauty of the divine. When we are moving a lot, when our thoughts are everywhere, and when we have no breath control, our experiences will remain shallow.

On maintaining depth in meditation:
- *Allow all emotions and feelings to arise.* Our emotions and feelings are a natural part of who we are as humans; we must not hold down or suppress feelings and emotions because they are uncomfortable. When we hold or suppress these things, it takes effort to hold them there, thus taking us out of full presence again, because we are expending effort to avoid certain emotion and feelings. We must allow all effort to stop.
- *Allow yourself to feel your energetic body expanding.* When we can feel into our energetic body, we will feel a sense of eternity, of unendingness; when we allow ourselves to know the eternal nature of our energy, the subtle colors and patterns of our soul and of deeper reality become perceivable.
- *Allow yourself to reach out with your feelings.* Instead of trying to manipulate things with our physical forms, we must learn to extend out with our energy. Feel yourself building

a relationship with your non-physical body, awakening a deeper knowledge and awareness of yourself.
- *Allow the divine energy of the universe to merge with you.* There is divinity all around us; there is pure energy all around us, waiting to be used. Call this divine energy into you, feeling it heighten your divine strength, emanating purity as you are filled with light.

On returning to presence:
- *Focus on the breath.* If we find ourselves back in the mind, we can bring our attention back to the breath, allowing the mind to slowly fall away once more.
- *Surrender all thought and worry.* Any line of thought or worry of life that takes you out of the present moment—simply surrender those thoughts to the universe. Allow yourself to give all worry unto the universe, know you are not your thoughts and that you are not defined by your thoughts.

XVI

Summary

Throughout these pages, we have covered many fundamental topics and concepts on the matters of self-awareness, spiritual awareness, and how our experiences of our early or recent life can create unconscious filters through which we view the world. We have gone over acknowledging these filters and how to release them and work through them, as well as releasing past experiences so that we may experience life as it is truly meant to be experienced. We took many concepts and philosophies and went over how they apply at the individual level as well as the collective level at the same time. We have discussed the importance of developing our own individual spiritual practice to begin carving away at the illusion that we have for millennia instilled upon ourselves and society.

We went over the fundamentals of duality, and how many of our modern problems stem from a lack of awareness about the nature of duality, and the mental limitations that it creates. We went over the fundamentals of shadow work, and what it truly means to be doing the deep inner work on ourselves. There are also many tools and questions

SUMMARY

that are written here that may be used to engage with ourselves on deeper levels of introspection and build the foundations of a shadow work journey.

It needs no emphasis that these words may be hard to hear for some. However, they are not meant to instill fear, negativity, or anything of the sort. These words have been organized in such a way as to inspire the interest in deep introspection and true self-knowledge beyond all perceived limitations and how to begin releasing these mental constructs and self-imposed prisons or limitations. These words, if basically grasped, can inspire us to learn about why we are the way we are. These words may serve as the beginning catalyst for an awakening of the divine essence within the human self. As with the beginning of this book, we asked the fundamental question, "Who are you?" It is a question that spiritual leaders, philosophers, and gurus have asked for many thousands of years. This answer is found only when all mental constructs and beliefs are let go. Only then may we know who we are beyond who and what we currently think we are. A healed world will require us to search ourselves and to know who and what we truly are. May these words assist all who read them in understanding this question, and then knowing the answer.

So shall it be.

About the Author

Jacob Goodson, born on May 10th, 1997, in Maryland, spent his formative years in Northern Virginia, experiencing the standard suburban life. Early life consisted of going to church on Sundays, as he was raised roman catholic. As well as going to school during the week and receiving average grades. As someone with a decent amount of friends and a social life, still he never felt he was one of the crowd, there was always a feeling of something missing. Never fully being understood or heard by friends or family led to poorly managed anger and emotional turbulence. Being forced to attend therapy that was unwanted and being sent to psychiatric hospitals only fostered deeper resentment within him. Not having the mindset for college, never having an interest in taking the SAT's, and at a loss for the next step of his life, Jacob decided to enlist.

His life took a turn after a four-year stint in the US Navy. Towards the end of his navy career, something started pulling him to start exploring meditation seemingly out of nowhere, as if it were whispered by a divine presence. Mystical visions of the depth of reality occurred while in these beginning meditations leading him to explore the profound depths of existence.

Through dedicated spiritual practice and years of coaching individuals through their own struggles, Jacob discovered his true calling as a spiritual guide. His expertise now serves to help individuals navigate personal growth and better their lives. Embodying the spirit of his book, *Awakening*, Jacob's journey exemplifies the transformative power of spiritual resilience.

JOURNAL ENTRIES

JOURNAL ENTRIES

JOURNAL ENTRIES

JOURNAL ENTRIES

JOURNAL ENTRIES

JOURNAL ENTRIES

JOURNAL ENTRIES

JOURNAL ENTRIES

JOURNAL ENTRIES

JOURNAL ENTRIES

Milton Keynes UK
Ingram Content Group UK Ltd.
UKHW021023130524
442628UK00016B/940